PRACTICAL PSYCHOMETRICS

Practical Psychometrics

A GUIDE FOR TEST USERS

Benjamin J. Lovett

THE GUILFORD PRESS
New York   London

Copyright © 2023 The Guilford Press
A Division of Guilford Publications, Inc.
370 Seventh Avenue, Suite 1200, New York, NY 10001
www.guilford.com

Printed in the United States of America

This book is printed on acid-free paper.

Last digit is print number: 9   8   7   6   5   4   3   2   1

Library of Congress Cataloging-in-Publication Data
Names: Lovett, Benjamin J., author.
Title: Practical psychometrics : a guide for test users / Benjamin J.
    Lovett.
Description: New York, NY : The Guilford Press, [2023] | Includes
    bibliographical references and index. |
Identifiers: LCCN 2022048285 | ISBN 9781462552092 (paperback) |
    ISBN 9781462552108 (cloth)
Subjects: LCSH: Psychometrics.
Classification: LCC BF39 .L69 2023 | DDC 150.1/5195—dc23/eng/20230222
LC record available at https://lccn.loc.gov/2022048285

To Alex Jordan, *a friend indeed*

Preface

I wrote this book to fill a gap—to try to explain the basics of psychometrics to the people who need that understanding most: *test users*. Professionals such as school psychologists, special educators, counselors, speech–language pathologists, and social workers sometimes administer tests and scales, or review evaluation reports with test data, and need to make sense of the test scores they see. My own students are preparing to become these kinds of professionals; most of them are in a master's degree program, getting trained to become practicing school psychologists. I had five goals for the book, and I knew of no other books that met those goals at the same time. Specifically, I wanted the book's content to be (1) accessible, (2) intuitive, (3) concise, (4) clinically relevant, and (5) technically accurate:

1. *Accessible*—Most test users have only minimal background, if any, in statistics and may be avoidant (even somewhat afraid) of mathematical material. Unfortunately, many psychometrics books assume statistically sophisticated readers and are stingy in providing clear and detailed examples. I aim to cover mathematical formulas only when necessary for understanding and to focus on conceptual descriptions.

2. *Intuitive*—I wanted test users not only to know (for instance) the relationship between the reliability coefficient and the standard error of measurement, but also to understand *why* the relationship makes sense. It's easy enough to present formulas and definitions; it's harder to show readers why these formulas and definitions are logical rather than arbitrary.

3. *Concise*—My students don't have time for a lengthy treatise exploring everything that we can do with measurement; the basics are enough, provided that those concepts are clearly learned and understood. Similarly, most test users (and those studying to be the same) can't devote a full semester to psychometric theory. Therefore, I aimed to write a book that could be used as a textbook for just several class periods and that could serve as a quick reference and resource for practicing test users who need to "study up."

4. *Clinically relevant*—Many psychometrics textbooks take the point of view of a test developer or researcher who is interested in large datasets. My students are training to be clinicians; they are interested in applying psychometrics to the individual client that they have in front of them. I have tried to use clinical examples throughout, referencing a variety of professions.

5. *Technically accurate*—When offering accessible and intuitive information about psychometrics in a concise format, it is tempting to "fudge" some of the technical niceties—to say things that aren't exactly accurate, oversimplifying the material. While writing, I sometimes felt that a psychometrician was looking over my shoulder, and I tried not to incur their disapproval too often.

Aids for Learning

I've incorporated a number of features into the book to make it more useful for instructors and for students as a learning tool:

- Most of the chapters end with a set of applied exercises. Some of the exercises give students an opportunity to calculate various test score data, but generally the exercises focus on interpretation of test scores. Many exercises ask students how they would respond to questions or concerns about tests, and they give students an opportunity to practice explaining psychometric ideas to various audiences (examinees, parents, etc.). In addition, I have provided suggested answers to the exercises in Appendix B of the book.

- In Appendix A of the book, I have written an annotated guide to more advanced books and even some journal articles on psychometrics.

Although I worked hard to make this book accessible and concise, that also meant recognizing that it's only a first step for students who want to do psychometric research or otherwise obtain more advanced skills.

- The appendices are followed by a glossary of key terms (including any term used in **boldface** in the book). This provides a ready reference for readers who might not always recall a term from an earlier chapter or who use the book primarily as a resource in which to look things up.

- In the final chapter (Chapter 8), I include excerpts from sample evaluation reports to show how to further apply the principles discussed throughout the book. This chapter is designed as an additional resource for students and professionals who are writing up test score data for their own reports.

Acknowledgments

First, it's a pleasure to thank my editor at The Guilford Press, C. Deborah Laughton, for her encouragement, guidance, and feedback throughout the process. I'm also so grateful to experts who reviewed the book for Guilford and provided feedback prior to publication: J. Gayle Beck, Matt Burns, Randy Floyd, and Laura Spenceley. It was Laura whom I first approached with the idea of this book in the Fall of 2020, and her reaction motivated me to actually write it! At Guilford, it was another Laura—Laura Specht Patchkofsky—who deftly handled production issues.

More generally, while writing this book, I often thought about the courses in psychometrics that I took as a student, and I'm grateful to Hoi Suen at Penn State and Brian Martens at Syracuse for the excellent foundation they provided. While they have very different instructional styles, both professors put an interesting behavioral spin on psychometrics, and I continue to use the models and metaphors they taught me. While in graduate school, my advisor, Larry Lewandowski, and my clinical mentor, Michael Gordon, showed me both the power and limitations of psychometric data, as applied to high-stakes decisions; they both served as additional inspiration for this book. Finally, for assistance with reviewing chapters, checking exercises, and formatting materials, I'm grateful to my Teachers College colleague Matt Zajic and my students Thea Bucherbeam, Tess Schaberg, and Lisa Szczesniak.

This book is the culmination of many years spent thinking about measurement. In some sense, I've been interested in testing and measurement since childhood. On the rainy days when I "played school" with friends as a child, I would actually make tests for others to take. At the age of 16, I discovered psychology and psychological testing, and when I learned that whole careers in assessment were possible, I knew that I would have one. For over 15 years now, I've been teaching psychometrics and psychological testing in classes for undergraduate and graduate students, and I've been giving workshops on assessment issues for test users such as psychologists, teachers, learning specialists, and counselors. It's been a genuine privilege to be able to do all this work and now to finally include some of my material in a book.

If you are an instructor, I hope that this volume serves your needs in the classroom, and if you are a student or a practitioner, I hope that you find this volume helpful in your work. If you have any comments or suggestions, please contact me at *BL2799@tc.columbia.edu.*

Contents

PRACTICAL PSYCHOMETRICS

CHAPTER 1

Introduction to Testing

Four Testing Stories

Tim Johnson's mother was not happy. She dropped Tim off at school herself and stopped his teacher just before class began. The scores from the Stanford Achievement Test had been sent home, and Ms. Johnson saw that Tim's reading score was at the 40th percentile. She handed the teacher the letter that had arrived the day before and said, "It's already February—if my son is failing reading, I should have heard about it by now!" The teacher found herself unsure about how to respond. She knew that Tim had no serious problems in reading—he was in the "middle of the pack" in her class—but she didn't know how to explain exactly what a 40th percentile score meant.

In the school's conference room, things were also a bit tense. Flavia Jimenez had been receiving services for a learning disability for a few years already, and the special education team was meeting to review the results of a recent reevaluation that would qualify Flavia to continue receiving services. The school district defined a learning disability as a gap between a student's IQ and their academic skills. Flavia had recently obtained an IQ score of 93, and her math score was 80, but this gap wasn't large enough to qualify as learning disabled. The school psychologist noticed that on one specific part of the IQ test, Flavia's score was 105 and wondered if this could be used as a comparison to the math score. The district's special education director was hesitant to make this comparison, while Flavia's resource room teacher expressed concern that one way or another, Flavia needed services for her problems with math.

The school psychologist was hoping to settle Flavia's case quickly; he was already thinking about a phone meeting that he had on his schedule at the end of the school day with a local audiologist who had diagnosed a student from the school with auditory processing disorder. The student, Casey Kellum, had apparently done poorly on diagnostic tests where she needed to repeat words that she heard played against a background of white noise. Casey was the fifth child at the school who had been diagnosed by this audiologist in the past year, and the school psychologist was beginning to grow skeptical about the diagnosis, while the administration was concerned about paying for electronic microphone equipment for yet another student with an auditory processing disorder diagnosis. The school psychologist was able to get the manual for the auditory processing test and was trying to figure out if its scores were accurate.

Eventually, the end-of-day school bell rang, and as the psychologist picked up his phone to place a call to the audiologist, another student at the school, Darius Leonard, got picked up by his father, who drove him to his weekly appointment with a mental health counselor. Darius had always been something of a "nervous" kid, and even though he was doing well enough in his classes, he had recently started to try to get out of going to school in the morning, claiming that he felt sick. At one point, he even lied to his father, telling him that the school was closed for the day. In his first visit with the counselor, the counselor asked Mr. Leonard to complete a rating scale concerning Darius's symptoms, and the scores suggested that Darius had significant anxiety problems. Mr. Leonard disputed this suggestion, saying that all kids worry about things, and he didn't see how this was unusual. The counselor knew that her scale could detect clinical problems, but she wasn't sure exactly *how* the scale did that. When she failed to explain the scoring process to Mr. Leonard, he rolled his eyes and reluctantly paid for counseling.

*   *   *

Although the specific details change a bit, I've seen each of the above situations happen multiple times. All of the situations stem from gaps in knowledge about *psychometrics*—the science that underlies psychological and educational measurement. I wrote this brief book as a primer for professionals who administer or interpret psychological or educational tests. Psychometrics has some mathematically sophisticated aspects, but thankfully, the average test user doesn't need to perform lots of mathematical calculations. Instead, most test users—teachers, school psychologists, speech-language pathologists, educational diagnosticians, counselors, and others—just need to be able to make informed judgments about which tests to select and how to draw conclusions and make decisions on the basis of the resulting test scores. At times, test users also need to be able to communicate with laypeople (such as clients and family members) about test data. All this does require some grounding in psychometrics—*practical* psychometrics, as I call it.

Psychometrics textbooks tend to be geared toward future researchers or test developers; these are important audiences, but most test users aren't well matched to these books and may not even have the background needed to understand the books. In contrast, this book makes no assumptions about your mathematical background and only expects you to *use* tests, just as most people in the fields of education, psychology, and related fields do. Throughout the book, the emphasis is on keeping things as simple as possible, while giving you the information you absolutely need to know to properly choose tests and interpret scores. There are applied exercises in most of the chapters, which allow you to try out your understanding. In addition, in Appendix A, I include an annotated list of resources for additional reading for those who are interested in more advanced study. But to better understand what's happening with Tim, Flavia, Casey, and Darius, some basic practical psychometrics is sufficient.

A Preview of the Book

Even with a focus on practical psychometrics, there's no way to avoid a bit of statistics, so the next chapter (Chapter 2) covers the statistical concepts that you absolutely need to know to go on. Chapter 3 then looks at test scores themselves. What does an IQ score of 110 really mean? Why are the SAT scores much higher numbers (e.g., 1200)? And why, in our opening example, was Tim's 40th percentile score no cause for great alarm? Chapter 4 examines reliability—the degree to which test scores are dependable and consistent. If Darius's score on that anxiety rating scale varied a lot from one day to the next, his father might be right not to trust it, so how can we tell just how reliable the score is? Chapter 5 examines validity, which is perhaps the most important quality in testing. A common way of summarizing the concept is that valid tests measure what they claim to measure: if Casey's audiologist is correct, the auditory processing test is likely a valid indicator of the disorder. Chapter 6 takes an in-depth look at a statistical procedure, *factor analysis*, that provides one way of investigating the validity of tests. Chapter 7 examines a timely issue in testing—how test developers and users ensure that tests aren't biased against examinees from different groups, and that the tests are used in a fair manner. Finally, Chapter 8 offers guidance about how to communicate test score information when giving feedback to examinees, holding conferences with families and other professionals, and writing formal evaluation reports.

Basic Terms in Testing

Throughout the book, I use examples of tests in different fields and professions. Some readers may not have completed any prior work in testing or may only be familiar with one particular type of test, so it is important to cover some basic terms.

I use the word *test* to refer generically to any standardized measurement procedure that leads to a numerical score. At times, I refer to *cognitive* or *performance* tests and measures, which are typically used to assess intelligence, academic skills, neuropsychological functioning, and speech and language development. These are sometimes called *measures of maximal performance* because they involve trying to get the examinee to give their best performance; they require some degree of effort to show the examinee's skills or competence. These tests typically involve tasks or questions that have right and wrong answers. Other "tests" are scales for the measurement of personality traits and psychological problems. These are typically structured questionnaires, rating scales, or standardized observation procedures. We might ask someone to complete a questionnaire about their anxiety symptoms, or we might ask a parent to complete a rating scale relating to their child's level of disruptive behavior. There's no "wrong" answer unless the person completing the scale is dishonest; two people could each be accurate and give very different answers. These tests are sometimes called *measures of typical performance* because they are supposed to show the examinees as they typically are, rather than catching the examinees at their best or worst. I refer to the both types of tests as *diagnostic tests* because they are being used for clinical purposes. They differ in important ways from typical teacher-made classroom tests. (Some of these differences are illustrated in later chapters.)

Any given test is usually made up of many different items, and often the items are grouped into *subtests*. For instance, an IQ test might have 10 different subtests, and each of the subtests would have its own set of items. One subtest might measure vocabulary knowledge, and each item on that subtest would be a question about a different word that the examinee needs to define. Another subtest might measure visual reasoning skills, and each item on that subtest would show the examinee a picture that has a part missing, which the examinee would need to identify. Typically, subtests will have separate numerical scores, and there will also be a *composite* or *index* score that describes performance totaled across multiple subtests. Rating scales and personality questionnaires also often have item groupings, sometimes called *subscales*, and they generate their own scores too.

Finally, when referring to people who are taking the test, or more generally the people whose behavior or performance is being assessed, I often use the generic term *examinees*. At times, I make more specific references to *students* or *clients* when I speak of examinees in particular settings such as schools or counseling centers. When referring to the person administering, scoring, and interpreting the tests, I use terms such as *examiner, evaluator, clinician*, and *practitioner*, and sometimes I mention particular types of professionals.

Tests as Assessment Tools

Life is filled with tests. Just a minute after being born, a baby is given an Apgar test based on their appearance and behavior; testing happens throughout the years of school and work; in old age we take tests measuring dementia, and sometimes tests of brain death are eventually given. It is no surprise that such a common feature of the world is also controversial, since important decisions often hinge on test scores. Readers may be familiar with the controversies that have arisen over the use of state achievement tests for children, college admissions tests for high school seniors, and the like. Controversies surrounding diagnostic tests are also common, and in clinical settings, practitioners are sometimes challenged by other professionals or by examinees and their families over the use of standardized tests. At other times, you will meet people who do the opposite, investing test scores with almost magical powers to predict someone's future performance or behavior without a chance of error.

Although I refer to the class of tests covered in this book as "diagnostic" tests, they are used for several distinct purposes. One, unsurprisingly, is *diagnosis*—that is, applying a formal, clinical diagnostic label. For instance, a child with intellectual disability is typically diagnosed as such in part on the basis of scores from an IQ test and from a measure of "adaptive behavior" (everyday life functioning). Similarly, scores from a standardized self-report scale of depression symptoms can be helpful when deciding whether or not to diagnose a client with major depressive disorder. A second purpose of these tests is *screening*—determining who needs a more thorough evaluation. Some tests are explicitly marketed as being for screening; they tend to be briefer, inexpensive, and more time-efficient. For instance, a brief intelligence screener can be used to rule out intellectual disability, and if a student obtains a low score, a complete IQ test can then be given. Similarly, for depression, a two-item questionnaire (the Patient Health Questionnaire–2) is used to quickly rule out major depressive disorder, or else suggest a need for a more comprehensive assessment (Li et al., 2007). A third purpose of these tests is *identification*; rather than relating to a formal clinical diagnosis, identification has to do with other types of classifications: various special education categories, a need for gifted support, high risk for a suicide attempt, and so on. Finally, these tests are sometimes used for *progress monitoring*—determining if an examinee's skills or traits are changing over time, especially in response to some type of remediation or intervention. A reading test may come in three versions, and the different versions can be administered over the course of a school year in September, February, and June, to determine whether a student's reading skills are improving.

It is important to keep in mind that diagnostic tests are nothing more than assessment tools; they are designed to gather information about examinees to help us make decisions or offer advice to try to help people. Tests are different from other assessment tools, such as unstructured interviews and observations, because they are highly standardized; they involve presenting stimuli in a standardized format (every examinee gets the same instructions and items), recording the examinee's responses according to standardized rules, and then transforming the responses into numerical scores that can be compared across examinees. Tests are no better or worse than other assessment tools; they have unique advantages and disadvantages, and so do the other tools. We don't ever make decisions based solely on test scores; if that could be done, there would be no need for clinicians, and technicians could simply administer and score the tests. Instead, practitioners always integrate information from a variety of sources. However, tests are a very important type of tool for making clinical decisions.

In sum, knowledge of psychometrics should demystify tests. Rather than viewing them, on the one hand, as perfect indicators or, on the other hand, as vessels of bias and abuse, competent practitioners view tests as helpful but fallible tools for learning more about an examinee. More importantly, knowledge of psychometrics allows you to make better decisions about which tests to use and about how much confidence you should have in your interpretations of those tests. Welcome again to the science of testing!

CHAPTER 2

Statistical Concepts

The statistics underlying test development are complex, and many research articles on psychometrics contain highly sophisticated statistical methods. However, only certain basic statistical concepts are needed to become a competent *user* of tests. In this chapter, my goal is to explain the statistical concepts needed to understand the psychometric principles covered in later chapters. Some readers will find this chapter to be a review of already-learned information; if so, feel free to skip to the next chapter, but it is often helpful to review and reinforce this foundational material.

First, though, we need to introduce a few important preliminary terms: a **sample** is a group of people for whom we have direct data—people who took a test or those who participated in a research study or test development procedure. A **population** is typically a much larger group containing all of the people who the sample is designed to represent. For instance, when test developers administer a language development measure to 100 3-year-olds to determine the typical level of language skills in children of that age, the 100 children are the sample, but the population might be all 3-year-olds in a particular country. Similarly, if researchers wish to compare adolescent boys and girls on a self-report questionnaire of depression symptoms, the researchers will obtain a sample of boys and girls who are to be given the questionnaire, but the data for the two groups are meant to represent the populations of adolescent boys and girls as a whole. **Descriptive statistics** aim to describe a sample, whereas **inferential statistics** tell us how confident we can be in making inferences about a population based on a sample.

Univariate Descriptive Statistics

When descriptive statistics are only about a single variable, they are called **univariate statistics.** Consider one such variable: a classroom test given by a college professor. The following scores (percent correct scores) came from a midterm exam that I gave many years ago in a class containing 24 undergraduate students:

97	75	84	55	91	100
87	96	88	69	81	81
59	69	95	61	97	91
86	88	94	91	52	57

We would call 24 our **sample size** (commonly symbolized as n or N).

Measures of Central Tendency and Dispersion

If you asked me how my students performed, you probably would not want to hear a listing of the 24 scores. Knowing this, I might tell you how the students performed "on average." An average, or **measure of central tendency,** allows us to describe a sample using a single value to represent the entire sample. Measures of central tendency also serve as a standard against which to judge any particular person's performance. As we will see in Chapter 3, most diagnostic tests define scores as high or low in relation to the average score (rather than in relation to some external standard).

The most common type of average is the **mean** (M), which is calculated by totaling all of the scores in the sample and dividing by the number of scores. The total sum of the 24 scores above (e.g., 97 + 75 + 84 . . .) is 1944, and 1944 divided by 24 is 81. The mean of those test scores is therefore 81; I can say that, on average, students got about 81% of the points available on the exam. Another common type of average is the **median,** defined as the middle value in a set of test scores ordered from lowest to highest. This means that about 50% of test scores in the sample will be below the median, and 50% will be above it. The median of the 24 test scores above is 86.5 because when there are an even number of test scores, the median will be halfway between the two middle values. Based on that median, I know that half of the class received a score above 86.5, and half of the class received a score below 86.5. A final type of average is the **mode**, defined as the most frequent score in a sample. The mode of the 24 test scores is 91, since three students received a 91, and no other score was received by more than two students.

How good a job does an average do, when it comes to representing a set of scores? In part, it depends on how variable the scores are. If everyone in my class had received an 81 on the exam, the mean (81) would be perfectly representative of the whole set of scores. But this is almost never the case; there is almost always some variability in the scores, and some sets of scores are more variable than others. **Measures of dispersion** quantify how variable a set of scores are.

The simplest measure of dispersion is the **range**; just as the word might suggest, the range is simply the difference between the highest and lowest scores in the set. In our set of 24 scores, the range is calculated by subtracting 52 (the lowest score in the set) from 100 (the highest score in the set); the range is 48. A more common measure of dispersion is the **variance**, an index of how far the different scores fall away from the mean. The variance is calculated by first computing **deviation scores** (each score minus the mean). Each deviation score is then squared to eliminate any negative values. The squared deviation scores are totaled up, and that total is then divided by the number of scores in the set.[1] In our dataset, the mean is 81, so we would calculate the deviation scores by subtracting 81 from 97 (16), from 75 (−6), and so on. If we followed the entire series of calculation steps (calculating all of the deviation scores, squaring them, summing the squares, and dividing by 24), we would find that the variance of these scores is 218. I mention these steps so that you'll have a sense of how the variance is calculated, but in practice clinicians never need to actually perform the calculation. What clinicians must know about the variance is that, all else being equal, larger variances suggest more spread-out scores. If all the midterm exam scores had been pretty close to 81 (the mean), then the variance would be much lower than 218.

A final, and very useful, measure of dispersion is the **standard deviation (SD)**. If you have already calculated the variance, it is easy to get the

---

[1] I am treating the score sets as populations for the purpose of calculating the variance. For samples, many researchers would divide the summed squared deviation scores by $n - 1$ (23 in this case) rather than n (24).

standard deviation: it is simply the square root of the variance. In our case, that is approximately 14.76. The standard deviation tells us how far away from the mean it is typical for a randomly picked score to fall. It is similar to the average deviation score. In our set of scores, the mean is 81, but it is common for scores to fall some distance away from 81, typically about 15 points away (on average).

Frequency Distributions

One way to represent both central tendency and variability is through a graph of a score set's **frequency distribution.** The graph, which is itself known as a **histogram,**[2] shows the frequency with which the score set has scores at each level (e.g., low scores, high scores). The score level is represented on the x-axis of the graph, and frequency is represented on the y-axis. Figure 2.1 shows the frequency distribution for the 24 scores listed earlier. On the x-axis, there are six columns, each representing a 10-point spread in test scores. On the y-axis, we can see which score ranges have more or fewer scores—that is, how many students earned scores in each range.

On many diagnostic tests, the histogram has a bell-like shape (also known as a *bell curve*) and it approximates a frequency distribution known as the **normal distribution,** which looks something like Figure 2.2. Just like in the earlier histogram, the height (y-axis) value at any point in the normal distribution tells us the relative frequency of people who fall at that level of the scale on the x-axis. If it helps, you can imagine the area under the curve being filled in with tiny dots, each of which represents a different person. You can see that in the normal distribution, most people cluster around the middle, and very few people have scores that are either very low or very high.

The normal distribution has been studied for centuries, and many natural traits follow this distribution. Consider height, for instance; if we were to sample 1,000 men from the general population, their heights would follow an approximately normal distribution, with most men in the middle (somewhere near an average of 69 inches in the United States) and fewer

---

[2] A histogram may superficially resemble a bar graph, but technically, bar graphs are used to measure the frequency of different natural categories rather than to split up a continuous variable into a set of groups. Accordingly, the bars in a bar graph do not touch.

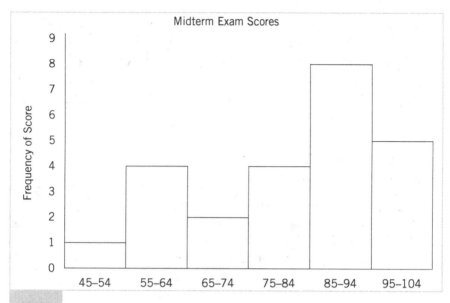

FIGURE 2.1. Frequency distribution of 24 test scores.

and fewer men appearing as we move farther away from the average in either direction. Diagnostic tests measure traits such as language ability and mathematics skills, and performance on these tests often follows a (roughly) normal distribution as well. Most scores are fairly close to the average score, and the score distribution is roughly symmetrical. Another helpful feature of any normal distribution is that the mean, median, and mode are all the same value, located easily as the highest point on the curve.

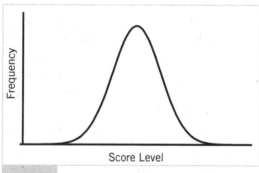

FIGURE 2.2. The shape of the normal distribution.

Two tests might both have normal score distributions, while having different means and standard deviations. Again, for U.S. men's heights, the mean is about 69 inches; for U.S. women's heights, the mean is about 63.5 inches. Men also have a larger standard deviation (National Center for Health Statistics, 2021). As we will see in Chapter 7, group differences also exist in score distributions for some diagnostic tests, but each group's score distribution is still typically normal in shape.

Statisticians know the math of the normal distribution well. In fact, there is a formula that will give the frequency (y-axis value) for any score (x-axis value) in the distribution. Clinical practitioners don't actually do any calculations with the formula, but we often use some rules of thumb to gauge how common or rare a particular test score is. A particularly helpful guideline is known as the **empirical rule**: it states that about 68% of scores in a normal distribution will be within 1 standard deviation of the mean score, about 95% of a normal distribution will be within 2 standard deviations of the mean, and about 99.7% of a normal distribution will be within 3 standard deviations of the mean. This can be seen most easily by looking at the histogram for the **standard normal distribution**, which is a normal distribution with a mean of 0 and a standard deviation of 1 (see Figure 2.3).

The added vertical lines in Figure 2.3 help to break up the area under the curve. About 68% of the area under the curve is between scores of –1

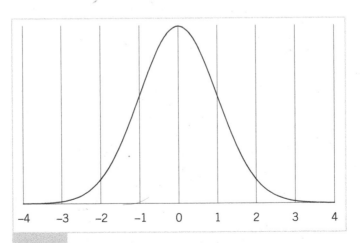

FIGURE 2.3. The standard normal distribution.

and 1 (i.e., within 1 standard deviation on either side of the mean). About 95% of the area under the curve is between scores of –2 and 2. And almost all of the area (about 99.7% of the area) is between scores of –3 and 3. These scores, which we will discuss in more detail in the next chapter, are known as *z*-scores: normally distributed scores with a mean of 0 and a standard deviation of 1. A handy feature of *z*-scores is that they tell you how many standard deviations away from the mean a score is. A *z*-score of 1.65 is 1.65 standard deviations above the mean; a *z*-score of –0.5 is one half of a standard deviation below the mean. All negative *z*-scores are below average; all positive *z*-scores are above average. Also, since the normal distribution is symmetrical, if 68% of the distribution is between –1 and 1, then half of that (34%) must be between –1 and 0, and the same amount between 0 and 1.

To see the utility of the empirical rule, consider another normally distributed variable, IQ. Its distribution is shown in Figure 2.4. The average (mean) IQ is 100, and the standard deviation is 15. Using the empirical rule, we know that about 68% of people have IQs between 85 and 115; about 95% of people have IQs between 70 and 130; and about 2.5% have IQs below 70, whereas the remaining 2.5% have IQs above 130. In Chapter 3, we will see more properties of normally distributed scores and discuss how to interpret an individual examinee's score using the normal distribution.

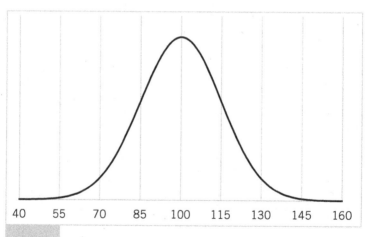

FIGURE 2.4. The IQ distribution.

Bivariate Descriptive Statistics: Correlation and Regression

Univariate descriptive statistics describe a single variable—its central tendency, dispersion, and frequency distribution. **Bivariate descriptive statistics** describe the relationship between two variables. These bivariate statistics underlie much of psychometrics.

The Correlation Coefficient (*r*)

Consider again the midterm exam scores that I used as an example earlier. Say that I wanted to see if performance on this midterm would predict how students would do on the final exam in the class. I would have two variables (the midterm exam and the final exam) from 24 students. One way to assess the relationship would be graphically, using a **scatterplot** where one variable is graphed on the *x*-axis and the other on the *y*-axis. (*Note:* This is *not* a histogram, and so frequency is not represented on the *y*-axis.) Each student's performance is plotted with *x* and *y* coordinates using the data from those two variables. I actually have the final exam scores for the same students, and I used those scores, along with the midterm scores, to make a scatterplot, where midterm values are on the *x*-axis and final exam values are on the *y*-axis in Figure 2.5. You can immediately see a trend in the data; generally, students who did better than their peers on the midterm also outperformed their peers on the final exam. This is typically described as a **positive correlation**: as one variable increases, the other does as well. Sometimes a pair of variables will show a **negative correlation**: as one variable increases, the other decreases. Perhaps if I surveyed the students to ask how many hours they had spent partying the week before the final, that variable would show a negative correlation with their final exam score!

Based on a scatterplot, a **regression line** or "line of best fit" can be calculated. This is the line that would come closest to all of the data points while remaining a straight line (technically, it's the line that does the best job of minimizing the sum of the squared vertical distances from the data points to the line). Figure 2.6 shows the same scatterplot as in Figure 2.5, but with the regression line added. As you might remember from high school algebra, the line has an equation, and you can use that equation, if you know someone's midterm exam score, to predict what their final exam score

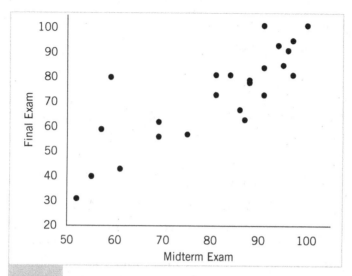

FIGURE 2.5. Scatterplot showing the relationship between students' midterm and final exam scores.

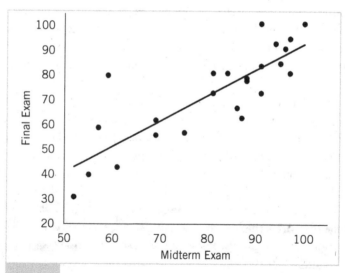

FIGURE 2.6. Scatterplot showing the relationship between students' midterm and final exam scores, with an added regression line.

is likely to be. For these data, the equation is $y = 1.0323x - 10.533$ (1.0323 is the slope of the line; −10.533 is where the line would intercept the y-axis when x is 0).

In psychometrics, we often want to know how strong the relationship is between two variables. This is typically quantified through the **correlation coefficient**. Technically, there are several types of correlation coefficients, but the most commonly used one is also known as a Pearson coefficient (it was developed by the statistician Karl Pearson) and symbolized by *r*. It examines *linear* relationships (relationships that look something like a *line* on a scatterplot). Pearson correlation coefficients vary between −1 and 1. An *r* of 1 represents a perfect positive correlation; all of the points are on a single line, and as one variable increases, so does the other. Such correlations are rare; an example would be the correlation between temperature in Fahrenheit and temperature in Celsius. An *r* of −1 would be a perfect *negative* correlation; again, all of the points are on a line, but as one variable increases, the other decreases. An example might be the relationship between the number of errors on a test and the score on the test. An *r* of 0 indicates no linear relationship between the two variables; knowing someone's score on one of the variables tells you nothing about their score on the other variable. As you can see from the example scatterplots and the *r*-values shown in Figures 2.7 through 2.10, in general, as *r* moves away from zero in either direction, the shape of the data on the scatterplot looks increasingly like a tightly clustered line. Incidentally, for the midterm and final exam data shown in Figure 2.5, the correlation coefficient is $r = .83$,

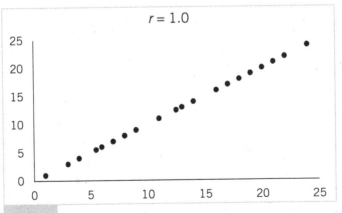

FIGURE 2.7. Scatterplot showing a perfect positive correlation.

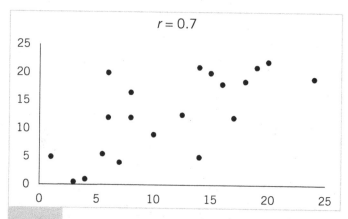

FIGURE 2.8. Scatterplot showing a strong positive correlation.

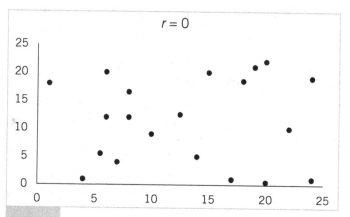

FIGURE 2.9. Scatterplot showing a null (zero) correlation, suggesting no systematic linear relationship between two variables.

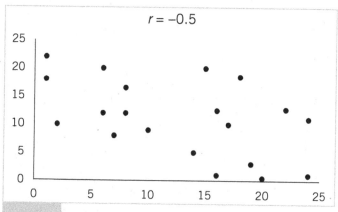

FIGURE 2.10. Scatterplot showing a negative correlation.

which is not perfect but still a very high positive correlation. At least in that course, for those students, midterm exam scores were a strong predictor of final exam scores.

Interpreting *r* Values

The correlation coefficient is so fundamental to psychometrics that it is worth delving into its interpretation in greater detail. One classic way to interpret r starts by squaring it. The squared correlation coefficient is also known as the **coefficient of determination** and is often described as indicating the proportion of variability in the predicted variable that is explained by variability in the predictor. Say that the SAT college admissions test is shown to correlate with college grades at $r = .50$. This would suggest that since $r^2 = .25$, one quarter (25%) of the variability in college grades is accounted for by variability in SAT scores, and the remaining 75% of the variability must be accounted for by other factors. This is a common way to interpret r, but it is does oversimplify things, and at times the size of r^2 can be misleading. For instance, aspirin has been shown to reduce the incidence of heart attacks, but in the famous large-scale study that led to this conclusion, the correlation between taking aspirin and having a heart attack was only $r = .034$, with $r^2 = .0011$. Taking aspirin explained less than 1% of the variability in who had a heart attack, but this does not mean that the effect was small; in fact, aspirin reduced the risk of a heart attack by almost one half! The low coefficient of determination only means that many other factors also affected whether someone had a heart attack, and most people in the study did not have heart attacks regardless of whether they took aspirin (see Rosenthal, 1990, for discussion).

This issue can be applied to psychometrics and testing as well. At times, the correlation between a psychometric test and an outcome is small—for example, $r = .10$. But when the outcome is an important one—say, a client engaging in a suicide attempt—even a small increase in our ability to predict the outcome can be very helpful. More frequently, correlations are in the range of .20 to .30, with the corresponding r^2 values between .04 and .09. Again, these seem small, but if a relatively brief diagnostic test can predict an additional 4 to 9% of the variability in school performance or mental health outcomes, this is a genuine contribution.

A second way to interpret r-values involves testing them for **statistical significance**, using inferential statistical procedures. Essentially, a test of statistical significance of *r* is designed to tell us how likely it is that we would see an *r*-value as high as (or higher than) the one that we observed in our sample, if in fact the "true" correlation in the entire population was 0. That likelihood is known as a **p-value**, where the *p* stands for probability—it is the probability of finding a relationship in a sample when there is no genuine relationship in the population as a whole. Smaller *p*-values are generally taken to indicate more confidence that the relationship observed in the sample is "real" (i.e., present in the population) and not just due to having an unrepresentative sample. By convention, a correlation coefficient is said to be "statistically significant" when its *p*-value is below .05. Say that you observe a correlation of .35 in a sample, and a statistical significance test shows that the *p*-value for this correlation is statistically significant, with *p* = .01. This means that there is only a 1% chance that you would observe a correlation coefficient $\geq .35$ in your sample, if in the population as a whole, the correlation was 0. Testing correlations for statistical significance is not always helpful in psychometrics because we are rarely interested in whether a relationship exists at all in the population; instead, we are interested in the size of the relationship. Moreover, statistical significance is determined mainly by *n*, the size of the sample being tested. With a high *n*, even very small correlations will be statistically significant, whereas in small samples, even strong relationships will not reach statistical significance. Despite these issues, test users should be familiar with statistical significance in correlations, since research articles almost always report this feature, and some test manuals do as well.

A third interpretive strategy, and one that is particularly useful in psychometrics, involves comparing the *r*-value that you observe to other *r*-values for similar measures. All measures are imperfect, and their correlation with outcomes is far from $r = 1.0$. Generally, when we are evaluating a test or other assessment tool, we want to know how it compares to other existing tools. If existing intelligence tests predict grades in elementary school at $r = .6$, and a new test can predict grades at $r = .7$, this is an improvement. If a new test can predict at $r = .6$ but the test is briefer than existing tests, that is also an improvement. Psychologist Jacob Cohen (1988) argued that more generally, when evaluating correlation coefficients, you should judge them as weak or strong relative to other correlations in the same field of research. Correlations are best described as high or low when compared to each other and when the set of correlations being compared involves the same or similar constructs. Cohen also noted that in fields such as psychology and education, $r = .10$ is generally considered a small relationship, $r = .30$ is generally considered of medium size, and $r = .50$ is large,[3] but he warned against applying these standards as rigid rules and recommended that professionals look to their own fields to see how a correlation compares to others in that field.

Regression Analysis

Earlier, we saw how any scatterplot has a line of best fit—a regression line—that can be used to predict someone's score on one variable, given the other. As the correlation rises (really, as it moves away from 0 in either direction), the regression equation becomes more useful. Psychometric researchers and test developers often use correlation and regression methods to predict one test score on the basis of another. For instance, how strong is the relationship between a child's reading speed and their reading comprehension skills? At other times, we might give the same test twice to the same group of examinees to see how stable it is. For example, if we give a questionnaire measuring anxiety symptoms to a group of clients referred to a waiting list for counseling and then administer the same questionnaire to that group 6 weeks later, how strong is the relationship in scores over time? As we will see in Chapters 4 and 5, correlation coefficients are central to studying the reliability and validity of tests.

At times, researchers and test developers need to look at the relationships between *multiple* predictors and a particular outcome. For instance, if we want to predict children's reading comprehension skills, knowing a child's oral reading speed is unlikely to explain all (or close to all) of the variability in reading comprehension, so we could also add information about the child's listening comprehension skills. We could ask whether those two predictors, together, allow us to predict a child's reading comprehension very well. To investigate this question, researchers use a procedure called **multiple regression**. It generates a **multiple correlation coefficient** (R, as opposed to the lower-case bivariate r), and the squared multiple correlation coefficient (R^2) tells us the proportion of variability in the outcome that the set of predictors taken together explains. In theory, more and more

---

[3]Some scholars have argued that correlations in the behavioral sciences tend to be smaller than Cohen had described, and so lower standards should be used (e.g., Funder & Ozer, 2019). However, in psychometrics, measures of certain constructs (such as intelligence and academic skills) will sometimes show quite high correlations.

predictors could continue to be added, and R^2 would keep growing until it eventually would become 1.0, showing that 100% of the variability in the outcome has been accounted for. In practice, only rarely are more than several predictors used at the same time.

Multiple regression has another advantage: it will also yield **standardized regression coefficients** (also known as *beta weights*, since they are often symbolized by the Greek letter beta, β) for each predictor. These "betas" indicate the strength of the relationship between each predictor and the outcome when all of the other predictors are controlled or held constant. For instance, in the example above, where reading speed and listening comprehension are the two predictors and the outcome is reading comprehension, the β value for reading speed would indicate the strength of the relationship between reading speed and reading comprehension *among children with the same level of listening comprehension skills*. Standardized regression coefficients are often consulted to indicate which predictors are more important than others. In addition, multiple regression analysis can be used to determine if adding a second predictor adds appreciably to predicting the outcome. If reading speed strongly predicts reading comprehension and adding listening comprehension doesn't change the R^2 value significantly, then listening comprehension may not be worth measuring in such a situation. This can be helpful information since practitioners often administer lengthy test batteries, and some of the measures may be superfluous. In Chapter 5, I will say more about *incremental validity*, the ability of a measure to add unique information over and above what is provided by other measures; this property is investigated using multiple regression.

Group Differences

Often, psychometric research examines group differences in test scores. Sometimes, this study is done to investigate a test's validity. For instance, a new measure of depression symptoms should yield higher scores in individuals with a prior, independent diagnosis of clinical depression than in nondiagnosed individuals. A validity study might check the existence and size of a group difference. At other times, test developers might want to know if people of different ages receive different scores, which would suggest a need for different score interpretation guidelines for different age groups. Finally, researchers may be concerned about the differential impact that test scores have on the treatment of examinees from minority groups, and so they might analyze ethnic group differences in test scores.

A number of statistical procedures may be used for analyzing group differences. Most of these procedures are inferential statistics, and they yield p-values. Therefore, a practitioner reading a research study or test manual can determine if the group difference is statistically significant. A p-value would indicate the likelihood of a group difference in a given sample happening just by chance, assuming that in the population as a whole no group difference exists. And just like p-values for correlation coefficients, the p-value for a group difference is highly dependent on the size of the sample; even very small group differences would be statistically significant in a very large sample. A p-value, therefore, doesn't give you a good sense of the *size* of a group difference, which is often what you'd like to know. To estimate the size of a group difference, an **effect-size** statistic is typically used. Perhaps the best known one is **Cohen's d**, also known as the **standardized mean difference**.

Cohen's d tells us how far apart the means of the two groups are in standard deviation units—that is, how many standard deviations away the means of the score distributions are. Consider a measure of expressive language skills that is given to two groups of children, one group with diagnoses of autism spectrum disorder (ASD) and one group of typically developing children. The score distributions of both groups have standard deviations of 10, but the typically developing group's mean score is 65 and the ASD group's mean score is 60. The two group means are 5 points apart, and each group's standard deviation is 10, so d is 0.5 (5 divided by 10); the group means are half a standard deviation apart.[4] Just as is the case with r-values,[5] d-values for group differences should be judged relative to other d-values in a particular area of research, but Cohen (1988) did offer a general rule of thumb: a d of 0.2 would generally represent a small difference, a d of 0.5 would be a medium-size difference, and a d of 0.8 would be a large difference.

It is useful to express group differences in standard deviation units (or other indices of the variability within each group) because this approach

---

[4]The calculation of d is somewhat more complicated when the two groups' standard deviations are not the same. You can use online effect-size calculators (e.g., *https://lbecker.uccs.edu*) to easily compute d if you know the groups' means and standard deviations.

[5]Technically, r is also a measure of effect size. In fact, there's even a formula to transform r to d and vice versa.

tells us the degree to which the two groups overlap. To see this, first consider the group difference situation shown in Figure 2.11. Groups A and B have means that are clearly different; Group B has a substantially higher mean. However, the two groups each have a lot of variability—that is, the standard deviations for the groups are fairly high—and so the two score distributions have a lot of overlap. Contrast this situation with the one shown in Figure 2.12. The mean difference between Groups C and D is the same as the mean difference between Groups A and B, but Groups C and D have much lower standard deviations, and so the two distributions have much less overlap. The effect size, d, would be much higher for the Group C–Group D difference than for the Group A–Group B difference, and this makes sense; two groups are more differentiated from each other when their standard deviations are lower.

Conclusions

Numbers are the language of psychometrics, and some basic statistical concepts are essential to understanding how tests work. Although the process of test development and psychometric research requires more advanced statistics, you can become a savvy consumer and user of tests by understanding a few selected concepts and knowing what to look for in test manuals and psychometric studies. Means and standard deviations, correlation

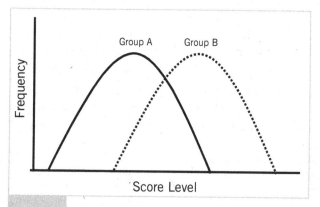

FIGURE 2.11. Two distributions with high variability (and therefore high overlap).

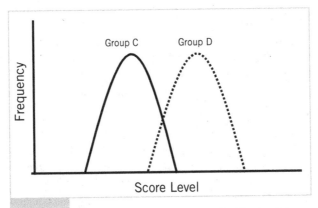

FIGURE 2.12. Two distributions with low variability (and therefore low overlap).

coefficients and regression analysis, and effect sizes for group differences are the most important concepts to start with in psychometrics. As you gain more experience and reinforce your statistical understanding, you'll become adept at interpreting these concepts when working with actual tests and making decisions based on an examinee's test scores.

APPLIED EXERCISES

1. A work colleague of yours has administered a diagnostic test and comes to you for advice. The colleague tells you that on the test that they administered, the scores have a mean of 50 and a standard deviation of 10, and they ask what that means. Explain in your own words what the standard deviation is, and use the empirical rule to help explain the implications of the standard deviation of 10 on that particular test, given that you also know the mean.

2. Consider a personality test that is used in counseling settings to offer vocational guidance. The test yields scores that indicate a client's "degree of match" with different jobs. The test developers followed 500 people to see what jobs they chose, and then they correlated the people's reported job satisfaction 6 months after starting work with the degree-of-match score that they had received for the job they were now working in. The correlation was $r = .60$, $p < .01$. How would you interpret this correlation, using the different techniques that were reviewed in this chapter?

3. On a test of early language development, a sample of 5-year-old girls receives a mean score of 85, whereas a sample of 5-year-old boys receives an average score of 78. Each group has a standard deviation of 18. What is Cohen's d for the gender difference in test scores, and how would a d-value of this size be interpreted? Moreover, say that a statistical test is performed on the data and that the group difference has a p-value of .08. How would this be interpreted?

4. Examine a manual for a diagnostic test in your field of practice. Locate the means and standard deviations for the different scores that an examinee receives on the test. Use the empirical rule to estimate how common different score levels are for those scores. Then check the "validity" section of the manual. If any correlation coefficients are reported, choose one and interpret it using the procedures discussed here. Moreover, see if any group differences are reported in the validity section, and if so, locate (or calculate) the d-values for those group differences.

CHAPTER 3

The Meaning of Test Scores

Thirty-six is the highest possible score on the ACT college admissions test, but 36 is also an extremely low IQ score. If you receive a 36 on a class midterm exam, you might be pleased if the score is out of 40 possible points, but you would probably be distressed if the 36 was out of 100. The same score carries very different meaning depending on the test's **scale**—the range and distribution of scores. This chapter covers common scales for different diagnostic tests and the ways that the resulting scores are interpreted.

Psychometricians make a broad distinction between two ways of interpreting scores. First, **norm-referenced score interpretations** involve comparison of different people to each other. A norm-referenced test score will tell the test user how the examinee performed or responded relative to other people. An IQ score is a typical norm-referenced score; an IQ of 100 doesn't mean that the examinee got 100 items right or 100% of the items right, but that the examinee performed exactly average for someone of their age, better than about 50% of people in their age group. Generally, norm-referenced tests are designed to show differences between individuals; if everyone received the same IQ score, the test would not be very useful. Norm-referenced tests are therefore useful for selection, classification, and similar decisions. Most diagnostic tests are norm-referenced, and most of this chapter will focus on them.

Another way of thinking about norm-referenced scores is that they tell us how common or rare someone's level of performance or functioning is. An IQ in the average range is, by the statistics of the normal distribution, very common. However, an IQ of 70 or below is exceedingly rare, obtained by only about 2% of people in the general population. In the same way, but in the opposite direction, an ACT score of 36 is quite rare, obtained by only the top <1% of the students taking the test in 2020–2021 (ACT, n.d.). Since norm-referenced scores tell us not just how one person did but how they did relative to others, the scores give us a good sense of whether the person's score was typical (near the average) or *unusually* high or low.

A second type of interpretation—a **criterion-referenced score interpretation**—involves the comparison of an examinee to an absolute standard (a criterion). A simple example would be the score from a road test used to license automobile drivers. Typically, the road test consists of a number of tasks, and errors cause the driver to lose points. If a particular road test has 100 possible points and scores of 90 and above are considered passing, the score of 85 has a direct interpretation compared to the mastery standard of 90; the hopeful driver has failed the test. Exams that school districts administer for school accountability are also criterion-referenced. The test developer or user sets standards for "proficient," "advanced," and other levels of skill, and a student is judged relative to those standards. If on a math test for eighth graders, scores of 525 and above represent proficiency in mathematics and scores of 566 and above represent advanced skills, a student who earns a score of 540 is thought to be proficient but lacks advanced skills in mathematics. A criterion-referenced score does not tell us how other examinees performed. If a school district implemented widespread instructional reforms that led to all eighth graders getting scores of 566 or above on the math test, the meaning of any individual's score would not change. Instead, the data would suggest that all eighth graders in the district now had advanced skills in math.

Test users often refer to norm-referenced and criterion-referenced *tests* or test *scores*. However, technically, it is the score *interpretation* that is norm- or criterion-referenced. For instance, the road test for the driver's license exam is typically interpreted in a criterion-referenced way, but if a city wishes to honor the most prepared young drivers, the Department of Motor Vehicles could identify those examinees who earned road test scores in the top 10% of those tested, interpreting the scores in a norm-referenced fashion. When I refer to norm-referenced tests or scores, I am referring to tests and scores that are typically (or designed to be) interpreted in a norm-referenced fashion. When I refer to criterion-referenced tests or scores, I am speaking about tests and scores that are typically interpreted in a criterion-referenced fashion.

Norm-Referenced Scores

Scores from diagnostic tests are typically interpreted in a norm-referenced fashion. One of the criteria for a clinical diagnosis (of depression, an expressive language disorder, etc.) is statistical rarity; we diagnose individuals whose trait levels are unusual in some way. If the trait is symptoms of anxiety, unusually high symptom levels might be part of the evidence underlying a clinical diagnosis of an anxiety disorder. If the trait is intelligence, unusually low levels of intelligence might be part of the evidence leading to a diagnosis of intellectual disability. Therefore, the core evidence involves comparing the examinee to other people to determine how unusual their responses are.

Who exactly is the examinee compared to on a norm-referenced test? The test is developed on a **norm group** (also known as a **standardization sample**). In the course of the test's creation, it is given to many people (often hundreds or thousands of people), and when the test is finally in applied use, each new examinee is compared to the norm group or a part of that group. The **norms** for a norm-referenced test show the distribution of scores in the norm group, so that a test user can find out if an examinee's score is average, unusually low, or unusually high. Often, the norm group is divided up into subgroups by demographic features, especially age. Therefore, if we are assessing mathematics skills in an 8-year-old child, we can compare their skills to those of just other 8-year-old children. Such a comparison group should always be specified, since the nature of the group can have a large impact on norm-referenced scores. I return to this topic later in the chapter, when discussing the importance of appropriate normative comparisons.

Norm-referenced scores are calculated by starting with an examinee's raw score. This might be the number of items they got correct on a reading comprehension test or the total number of points they earned on an essay test where the essay was scored out of 20 possible points. A raw score on a personality/psychopathology measure could be the number of symptoms that the examinee reported having, or the number of statements that they answered "yes" to. The examinee's raw score is then compared to the distribution of raw scores in the appropriate norm group block (which might be the people of the same age as the examinee) to check where their score is in relation to the average score of people in the block. Based on where the examinee's score falls within that distribution, it is transformed to a norm-referenced score. For instance, if the examinee's raw score on an IQ test (i.e., the points they earned for correct answers across all of the items) is at the exact average for their age group, the examinee will be assigned a norm-referenced IQ score of 100, since 100 is defined as the average IQ score at every age level. A norm-referenced score of 100 does *not* mean that an examinee earned 100 points; this score merely means that the examinee's IQ test performance was at the exact average of the score distribution for people of their age who were in the norm group.

Percentile Ranks

Perhaps the most useful norm-referenced scores are **percentile ranks** or percentile scores (sometimes abbreviated as %ile). They tell us what proportion of the population the examinee scored above. For instance, a student who scores at the 66th percentile of a test scored higher than 66% of the norm group, and the norm group is expected to represent the population. A score at the exact average[1] would be at the 50th percentile, and the average *range* is often taken to extend from the 25th to about the 75th percentile; thus, it is the middle 50% of the population. Many rating scales of attention-deficit/hyperactivity disorder (ADHD) symptoms suggest that a score is clinically significant if it is at the 93rd percentile or above—that is, if someone's symptom levels are in the top 7% of the population. The IQ cutoff for intellectual disability is at approximately the 2nd percentile; if a student has an IQ score in the bottom 2% of the population, that is part of the evidence needed for a diagnosis of intellectual disability.

Virtually all norm-referenced tests yield percentile ranks, along with other types of norm-referenced scores. Percentile ranks are easy to understand and to explain to clients, students, and families of children being assessed. Thinking in terms of proportions is intuitive, and laypeople understand why it is unusual that someone's test responses place them in, for instance, the top or bottom 5% of the population. However, on tests of academic skills, percentile ranks are sometimes confused with *percent correct* scores. A parent may hear that their daughter is at the 60th percentile in mathematics and think that the girl is almost failing (as a 60% class grade would suggest), when in fact she is doing better than most of her peers. Make

---

[1] Technically, the 50th percentile is the median, but in a normal distribution, the mean and median are the same.

sure to explain the difference between percentile rank and percent correct scores when presenting the percentile rank.

You need to consider two more technical caveats when interpreting percentile rank scores. First, they are not on an "equal interval scale"—that is, the difference in trait levels between (for instance) the 10th and 20th percentiles is not the same size as the difference between the 30th and 40th percentiles. Recall that in the normal distribution, most people are relatively close to the average, and the farther that you move away from the average, the fewer people you will find. Percentiles tell you how an examinee compares to other people, so percentiles will be clustered tightly near the average but will be spread out far at the edges of the distribution. The anxiety level of a client with an extremely high anxiety score (at the 99th percentile) might decrease substantially and still be at the 95th percentile. Meanwhile, if a client was at the 60th percentile to begin with, even a small (and clinically meaningless) decrease in anxiety might knock them down to the 50th percentile.

Given this caveat, note that you cannot perform meaningful arithmetic operations on percentile ranks. Calculating the mean of three different percentile rank scores is not accurate, for instance. Relatedly, you cannot meaningfully interpret the size of a gap between two percentile ranks without knowing the exact percentiles that the gap is between. To say, for instance, that a student increased 10 percentile rank units in reading comprehension between September and January of the school year could represent either a small or a large degree of growth depending on where along the normal distribution the growth occurred. Similarly, to say that one student is 10 percentile rank units above another student is not inherently meaningful. More information (such as the exact percentiles) can be helpful, but other types of norm-referenced scores that *do* have equal intervals are preferable for these purposes. In fact, many of the other norm-referenced scores that we cover are treated as having equal intervals.

There is yet a second caveat: in the norm-referenced scores that follow, I give percentile rank equivalents, but those equivalents assume an approximately normal distribution. Many score distributions, particularly for performance tests (cognitive and achievement tests), have approximately normal distributions, especially in children and adolescents. However, some neuropsychological tests do not (since almost everyone without brain damage does well), and many rating scales of clinical symptoms and problem behaviors also do not (since most people receive low raw scores, showing few symptoms, while those with clinical problems are spread far into the high end of possible raw scores). On tests with non-normal distributions, percentile ranks are particularly important, and they will not match up exactly with other types of scores. However, Figure 3.1 shows the expected relationships between the scores for normally distributed data.

z-Scores ($M = 0$, $SD = 1$)

We first encountered **z-scores** in Chapter 2, since these scores serve as landmarks along the normal distribution. A z-score tells us, quite literally, how many standard deviations away from the mean a score falls. If a counselor uses a norm-referenced scale to measure a client's level of anxiety and the client has a z-score of 0, the counselor knows that the client's reported anxiety level is exactly average, since the score is 0 standard deviations away from the mean. Negative z-scores are below the mean, whereas positive z-scores are above the mean. And almost everyone will have a z-score between –3 and +3. These features give z-scores some intuitive appeal to test users who understand psychometrics, but very few norm-referenced diagnostic tests actually use z-scores for their primary reporting method. I suspect that this

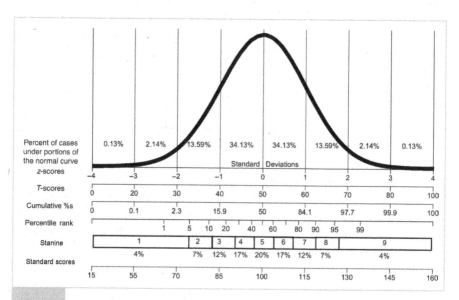

FIGURE 3.1. Normal distribution with norm-referenced score scales shown. From Bandalos (2018, p. 31). Copyright © 2018 The Guilford Press. Adapted by permission.

is because these scores are difficult to explain to laypeople. A score of 0 sounds like the examinee didn't get any items correct (or didn't report any symptoms), and a negative score is even harder to explain. Even so, z-scores are important for practitioners to know about, both when reading research articles and when thinking about how scores on different tests compare to each other. Indeed, z-scores provide a common metric for comparing the other types of norm-referenced scores presented in this section. If you are looking at scores from a battery of diagnostic tests, each of which uses a different type of norm-referenced scores, you can still think about the various scores that an examinee received as being, for instance, about half a standard deviation below the mean, two standard deviations above the mean, and so forth.

Standard Scores (M = 100, SD = 15)

Standard scores are common scores on tests of cognitive abilities, academic skills, adaptive behavior, language functioning, and related areas. They are used for the famous IQ test scale. Standard scores have an average (mean) of 100 and a standard deviation of 15, so a score of 70 is 2 standard deviations below the mean ($z = -2.00$) and an IQ of 70 is typically the cutoff for intellectual disability (the condition formerly known as mental retardation). On any given test, 68% of the population will have standard scores between 85 and 115, and 95% of the population will have scores between 70 and 130. The more you work with standard scores, the more you will develop an intuitive feel for what counts as a "high" score, a "bad" score, and so on. In particular, it is helpful to know the percentile ranks of common standard score landmarks: a standard score of 70 is at the 2nd percentile, a standard score of 80 is at the 9th percentile, a standard score of 90 is at the 25th percentile, and so on.

Subtest Scaled Scores (M = 10, SD = 3)

Many intelligence tests and measures of adaptive behavior (used to assess individuals with developmental disabilities) have subtests that use "scaled scores" with a mean of 10 and a standard deviation of 3. On this scale distribution, scores between 8 and 12 typically constitute the average range, being between the 25th and 75th percentiles. However, keep in mind that making important clinical decisions or other bold interpretations based on a single subtest can be hazardous, so make sure to examine the reliability and validity evidence for the specific subtests being interpreted.

T-Scores (*M* = 50, *SD* = 10)

T-scores are fairly common,[2] used in some cognitive ability and neuropsychological tests as well as many measures of psychological disorders. Behavior rating scales for children often use *T*-scores, as do clinical personality tests (e.g., the Minnesota Multiphasic Personality Inventory). Because they have a mean of 50, *T*-scores can be mistaken for percentiles, but they are actually very different. They are on an equal-interval scale, and because their standard deviation is 10, if the scores are normally distributed, almost all people will have scores between 20 and 80. Earlier I mentioned the ADHD symptom rating scales that use a 93rd percentile cutoff for clinically significant symptom levels. Most of these scales generate *T*-scores, and the cutoff is $T = 65$ (1.5 standard deviations above the mean, which is the 93rd percentile).

Stanines

Many achievement tests also have another type of norm-referenced score, the **stanine**. The stanine scale divides the normal distribution into 9 score ranges, with 5 being the middle range (the middle 20% of the distribution, incidentally), 1 the lowest, and 9 the highest. Typically, stanine scores of 4, 5, and 6 are considered the average range (together, they represent a bit more than the middle 50% of the distribution), with below-average and above-average scores being below and above that range, respectively. The stanine does not have any unique advantages over other norm-referenced scores, but because it only has 9 score ranges, some test users may find it simpler to interpret.

Age-Equivalent and Grade-Equivalent Scores

On tests in the areas of intelligence, academic skills, and speech/language, test users often have the option of recording **age-equivalent** and

---

[2] *T*-scores do not have anything to do with the *t*-test, an inferential statistic that is used for comparing two groups.

grade-equivalent scores. Also known as *developmental scores*, they are highly controversial. They are popular with some test users, but many scholars argue that they are so misleading that they do more harm than good.

If a student receives a grade-equivalent score of 5.3 on a test of reading skills, this is supposed to indicate that the student performed at the same level on the test as the median child in a sample of children in the third month of their fifth-grade year. Similar notation is used for age-equivalent scores; a child with an age-equivalent score of 8–11 is assumed to have performed like the median child in the norm group who is 8 years and 11 months old. Already there's one problem with this kind of definition: there may not be any children in the norm sample who were tested in exactly the third month of fifth grade, and so test developers might need to examine the scores of students at other developmental points nearby and infer where a child in grade 5.3 should perform. This process, known as *interpolation*, assumes that skills increase the same amount each month, which isn't necessarily the case.

Bigger problems with developmental scores come with misuse; not only is their official definition problematic, but many people interpreting the scores go far beyond that definition. For instance, if the student receiving a grade-equivalent score of 5.3 was just starting sixth grade (6.0), a teacher or parent might express concern that the student was "almost a year behind his peers," but in fact this would be inaccurate. It is common for a class of students to show fairly wide variability in academic skills, and so a grade-equivalent score of 5.3 likely puts the child near the average for their peers in that class. Such a misinterpretation also assumes that the scores are perfectly reliable, which is never the case (an issue discussed in detail in Chapter 4). Another common-but-incorrect interpretation is that the student reads the same way as students in the third month of fifth grade do. That assumes that the items on the test and the way that they're scored include all relevant aspects of the reading process, when they probably don't. Students of different age and grade levels will approach test items in different ways, even if their final scorable response is the same. Finally, some test users might infer that a student should be retained or given remedial instruction, or instead placed in a more advanced instructional setting, based solely on developmental scores: "He reads like a fifth grader, so why are we making him take sixth-grade reading lessons?" In fact, these are complicated decisions requiring far more information than someone's developmental score.

Each of these limitations applies equally to *age*-equivalent scores.[3] For these reasons, I cannot endorse the use of developmental scores, except in rare situations where the limitations of the scores are made clear. Other norm-referenced scores are easier to interpret and do not have all of these limitations to the same degree. Still, it is very important for test users to know about these scores; you will see them in practice, and you should know their limitations.

Transforming Norm-Referenced Scores

Figure 3.1 shows how several of the different norm-referenced scores relate to each other along the normal distribution. Extending a vertical line at any point along the distribution on the figure will show all of the norm-referenced scores at that point. In addition, you can find a "psychometric conversion table" on the internet to help with these transformations. Finally, if you are seeking a percentile rank and cannot find one, you can use an online calculator to transform whatever kind of score you have into a *z*-score, and then find out what percent of the population is below that *z*-score (i.e., the percentile rank) here: *www.calculator.net/z-score-calculator. html.*

What's Normal? What's Not?

In clinical assessment, regardless of the field, practitioners are typically focused on the question of whether a patient, client, or student is experiencing problems to an unusual degree. One criterion for a clinical diagnosis or a determination that clinical or educational services are needed is *statistical deviance*, or *deviance from the norm*.[4] Problems are present to a clinical degree in part because they are unusual. Norm-referenced tests can be extraordinarily helpful in these cases, but the term *unusual* is obviously ambiguous. There is no single point where someone's level of functioning

---

[3] The two types of scores (age-equivalent and grade-equivalent) also can lead to different conclusions, particularly among older students. As I discuss in more detail below, this is particularly problematic when assessing college students and other adults.

[4] Statistical deviance is not sufficient for a clinical designation, but it is one criterion. Typically, such a designation also requires functional limitations—that is, difficulties in everyday, real-world functioning of some kind, or at least significant distress.

suddenly goes from being normal to being abnormal. To take a medical example, if a systolic blood pressure of 140 is the cutoff for hypertension, this does not make a blood pressure reading of 139 perfectly fine!

Acknowledging that there is an element of arbitrariness in any cutoff for the "abnormal" range, we see that there are two sources of such cutoffs. The first is found in legal and policy regulations. For instance, perhaps a governmental agency decides that to be eligible for early intervention services, preschoolers must score below the 20th percentile in at least one area of development. When regulations define cutoffs, clinicians can easily cite and follow them. The second source of cutoffs is trickier to follow consistently: the narrative descriptions of test score ranges found in diagnostic test manuals. Test developers genuinely try to be helpful to practitioners by offering narrative descriptions such as "below average," "extremely low," "at risk," and "borderline clinical," but the terms and cutoffs differ from one test to another. A universal score interpretation system (Guilmette et al., 2020) has recently been proposed, but the current situation is unlikely to change quickly, since test publishers, test authors, researchers, and clinicians would all need to "get on the same page."

Earlier, as I was discussing the various norm-referenced score types, I mentioned some of the typical cutoffs for different tests. First, on measures of performance (e.g., cognitive, academic, neuropsychological tests), the "average range" is generally considered to be scores from the 25th up to the 75th percentile, which (in normally distributed scores) works out to standard scores between 90 and 110. (Sometimes, you will see the 74th percentile or a standard score of 109 used as the upper bound of the average range.) Many tests describe the 10 standard score points on either side of this range as "low average" and "high average." The idea is that standard scores between 80 and 90, and between 110 and 120, are not grossly deviant from average. Less than 20% of the population has standard scores either below 80 (which is at the 9th percentile) or above 120 (which is at the 91st percentile). On IQ tests, scores in these ranges are often referred to as "low" (on one side) or "superior" (on the other). Cutoffs even farther from the average are often described as "extremely low," "very superior," and so on.

On rating scales for psychopathology, high scores typically indicate higher levels of symptoms (i.e., more severe problems). Below-average and average range scores are generally viewed the same way, as simply indicating a lack of clinically significant problems. The cutoff for clinical significance is typically at either 1.5 standard deviations above the mean ($z = 1.5$, $T = 65$, or the 93rd percentile), or at 2 standard deviations above the mean ($z = 2.0$, $T = 70$, or the 98th percentile). At times, a lower standard (at $z = 1.0$ or 1.5) is used to define an "at-risk" threshold, suggesting a higher likelihood of problems developing.

Issues in Norm-Referenced Score Interpretation

The Importance of the Norm Group

On any norm-referenced test, the biggest determinant of the score is the group of people to which someone is being compared—that is, the norm group. Therefore, a key indicator of test quality is a good norm group, and a key to valid test interpretation is appropriate norms.

Size is one feature to look for in norm groups; all other things being equal, larger norm groups are better than smaller norm groups. However, what is most important with regard to size is *not* the norm group size as a whole (i.e., the total number of people included in the test development sample); it is the size of individual norm group *blocks*—the groups of people against which an individual's scores are compared. For instance, consider an IQ test that has been normed on 2,000 people—an impressive accomplishment! Dakin, a boy who is 8 years and 6 months of age, will not be compared to all 2,000 people; instead, he may only be compared to 100 children in the norm sample who are between 8 years, 5 months, and 8 years, 8 months, of age. It certainly makes sense to compare him to close age peers, but 100 is a far less impressive comparison group than 2,000. Tests with larger norm group blocks are preferred, regardless of the total sample size.

Representativeness is another important norm group feature. Generally, in the United States, norm groups are sought to be representative to the general population of the country. Often, test manuals will compare the demographic characteristics of the norm group to statistics from the U.S. Census, with particular regard to gender, ethnicity, and geographical location. For instance, if 85% of the people in a norm sample were men, this would vastly overrepresent men relative to their proportion in the general population. At times, age is another demographic factor matched to the Census, although on many tests, there are separate norms by age, making this type of matching unnecessary. In any case, test users should review the characteristics of the normative sample described in the test manual to ensure reasonably representative norms.

A final important norm group feature is *recency*. The average level of traits sometimes changes over time in a population. Therefore, all other things being equal, a test with more recent norms is preferable to one with older norms. For instance, to infer that a student's reading skills are at the 80th percentile relative to age peers, it is always most helpful to use a test where those peers (from the norming sample) were tested recently. Even IQ tests have shown average raw score performance changes over time, and so measurement of intelligence is most accurate when an examinee is compared to a norm sample from recent years. This is one reason why most diagnostic tests are revised and renormed every decade or so.

Norms Based on Demographic Groups

At times, test users have the option to compare someone's score to a group other than the general population or age peers.

Gender-Specific Norms

On many questionnaires and rating scales that measure emotional and behavioral problems, as well as personality inventories, norms are available (and are sometimes *only* available) by sex/gender. It can seem attractive to use gender-specific norms. For instance, when rating a young boy's level of hyperactivity symptoms, it might seem fair to compare him to other boys rather than all children his age, since boys are thought to be "naturally" more hyperactive. This comparison would avoid unfairly penalizing him for being a boy and risking pathologizing his typically male behavior.

From a diagnostic point of view, however, gender-specific norms have significant limitations. By definition, they erase actual gender differences in the traits they measure. For instance, if the 93rd percentile (e.g., a *T*-score of 65 or above) is the cutoff for clinically significant anxiety symptoms, gender-specific norms will make it so that 7% of males *and* 7% of females would meet clinical significance. But in fact females have far higher rates of clinically significant anxiety, often experiencing anxiety disorders at twice the rate of males (Hartung & Lefler, 2019). Similar gender differences (in both directions) are present for many other disorders and personality traits.

These differences can only be seen in norms that combine data across gender identities.

Gender-specific norms are also difficult to apply to the increasing number of clients who identify as transgender or nonbinary. In the case of transgender clients, using norms for the gender corresponding to their gender identity does not always work, particularly for children. When working with clients who identify as nonbinary, if a test only has gender-specific norms, it is best to score the test using both sets of norms and to view the client's true scores as lying somewhere between the two options (since that is what combined norms would yield). More generally, combined norms are to be preferred where they are available, except in specific cases where behavior relative to gender expectations is relevant.

Education-Group Norms

On many cognitive and achievement tests, norms are available not just for different age groups but also for different grade levels. A 12-year-old in sixth grade can be compared to other 12-year-olds or other sixth graders. Through the childhood and adolescent years, age- and grade-based norms yield similar scores for most examinees, the exception being students who are significantly older or younger than most people in their grade year. For individuals in late adolescence and adulthood, age and education norms often yield vastly different scores, since a significant proportion of the population does not attend higher education for long, if at all (Harrison et al., 2019). Comparing a 22-year-old college senior to other college seniors is quite different from comparing that student to all fellow 22-year-olds. Comparing a 25-year-old medical student to other students in their third year of graduate/professional school is *extremely* different from comparing the student to all 25-year-olds in the general population. Higher-ability individuals are more likely to seek more education and to be successful in their applications to education settings; moreover, education directly increases cognitive and academic skills.

Generally, for diagnostic and other clinical purposes, age norms are preferred, even in childhood, and they are certainly the most appropriate norms in older clients. However, educational norms can be helpful for making recommendations and inferences about a student's likelihood of success in various educational settings, and so they may be helpful to calculate when offering advice or counseling regarding educational placement decisions.

Norms Based on Race, Ethnicity, and Cultural Background

Many neuropsychological tests yield scores that are normed based on race or ethnicity as well as age, education, and gender. The original rationale for *race norming* was that neuropsychological tests were designed to assess the organic, biological effects of brain injury or degeneration, and the standard against which the examinee should be judged is that of their cultural peers, to eliminate the influence of cultural factors. Arguably, race norming could also affect the identification of students for special education services; currently (without race norming), a higher proportion of African American students are identified than other groups, although this appears to be explained by differences in academic performance and other factors besides race per se (Morgan et al., 2017).

Race norming is a controversial practice. Most recently, it has made news for its use in identifying neurological impairment among football players seeking compensation for play-related injuries (Associated Press, 2021). For clinical diagnostic decisions, combined norms are generally preferred, although in cases where the diagnosis depends on a decline in neuropsychological functioning, race norming continues to be used in some settings. As a consumer of evaluation reports, be careful to note whether any neuropsychological testing you review mentions "demographically corrected" norms, as they will likely include race, and this should affect your interpretation of the scores. Specifically, African American examinees may have significant increases in their scores on neuropsychological or cognitive tests in the presence of race norming, relative to the scores obtained with combined norms.

Extremity in Composite Scores

One of the most confusing situations for a practitioner involves a composite test score that is farther from the average than any of the scores making up the composite. For instance, consider a test of children's oral language skills, with a total language score made up of two subscores: one in expressive language (speech) and one in receptive language (listening). A child receives the following scores (on the standard score scale):

$$Expressive\ Language = 82$$
$$Receptive\ Language = 78$$
$$Total\ Language = 73$$

If the child's overall language skills are, in some sense, an average of their expressive and receptive language, why isn't the total score in the middle of the other two scores? At times, these phenomena lead to composite scores that meet clinical cutoffs for severe deficiencies, when none of the subscores making up the composite meet the cutoff. In these cases, it can be difficult to explain the situation to clients, families, and administrators.

Remember that norm-referenced scores tell you how rare a score is. In the above example, the Expressive Language score (82) is at the 12th percentile, meaning that only 12% of the population had lower scores than that. The Receptive Language score (78) is at the 7th percentile, so only 7% of the population had lower scores. A composite score based on those two subscores must consider how rare it is to have significant deficits in expressive *and* receptive language. This is rarer than just a single low score in one area of language.[5] Therefore, the composite score will be lower than either of the subscores that make it up. The Total Language score of 73 is at the 4th percentile, suggesting that only 4% of children have such poor overall language skills.

Whenever both (or all) of the subscores are on the same side of the mean, the composite will not be in the middle of the subscores—it will be farther from the mean than the average of the subscores. The degree to which the composite will be more extreme will depend on how correlated the subscores are, but some amount of composite extremity is the rule, not the exception. This occurs in either direction from the mean and should be expected, and it should be explained to clients and others in terms of the rarity of having multiple areas of functioning (the subscores) that are below (or above) average.

Base Rates of Extreme Scores in Batteries

We just saw how multiple extreme scores are rarer than a single extreme score. Relatedly, the more tests (or subtests) that are given, the more likely it is that an extreme score will be found somewhere in the battery. This can occur just by chance, or a few extreme scores in a lengthy battery can

---

[5]Consider the chance that there will be a hailstorm tomorrow in the city where you live. (The probability is likely relatively low.) Now consider the chance that there will be a hailstorm tomorrow *and* another hailstorm the day after tomorrow. That probability is even lower. The same is true of the probability of one low test score versus *two* low scores.

indicate genuine but very narrow strengths and weaknesses. Regardless, it should not be seen as unusual or statistically deviant to see individual extreme scores in batteries.

Recent studies have tried to quantify the *base rate* (the general population prevalence) of individual extreme scores—in particular, extreme low scores—using the data from normative samples of major diagnostic tests. The base rates have been found to be quite high. For instance, in one of these studies, Brooks (2010) found that *most* children in the normative sample of the Wechsler Intelligence Scale for Children (the fourth edition, the WISC-IV) had at least one subtest score that was at the 16th percentile or below. Almost half of the normative sample (43.4%) had at least *two* subtest scores meeting that criterion. Similar findings have been published regarding other tests.

The results of these studies have important clinical implications. First, avoid going on "fishing expeditions," evaluating a client in areas where there is no referral concern. If you keep assessing different areas, an apparent problem will "turn up," where or not it is meaningful. Second, and relatedly, insist on evidence beyond norm-referenced test scores before diagnosing a problem as a disorder or disability. The additional evidence might come from real-world (nondiagnostic) tests, clear self-reports and informant-reports, structured clinical observation, and so on. Finally, seek converging evidence from multiple diagnostic tests of similar areas of functioning to ensure that apparent problems are not just a statistical fluke.

Conclusions

Diagnostic tests generally provide norm-referenced scores that describe someone's functioning relative to a group of people on which the test was developed. Different types of norm-referenced scores look quite variable, but they can all be equated with percentiles, which is easy to do when the score distribution of a test is approximately normal. Moreover, a particular z-score always corresponds to the same T-score, standard score, and so on. When deciding how to interpret norm-referenced scores, keep several principles in mind. First, be sure that the norm group is reasonably large and representative of the population it is supposed to embody. Second, avoid norms based on particular demographic groups (other than age) except in unusual circumstances. Third, understand the relationshipt between subtest and composite scores, and why composite scores can sometimes be more extreme than any of the subtest scores making up the composite. Finally, be aware of the base rate of extreme subtest scores, and demand additional evidence to validate interpretations of these scores.

APPLIED EXERCISES

1. Consider the test scores for an adolescent undergoing a psychoeducational evaluation at school, shown in Table 3.1. Where do these scores fall relative to the average range? (You can assume a roughly normal distribution for this exercise.) What kinds of problems appear to be present? What areas of functioning are unimpaired? What areas of functioning are perhaps *better than typical?* To help justify your answers, describe the (approximate) percentiles of these scores.

2. At a special education committee meeting one day in June, the school principal points out that Briana's age-equivalent language development score is a year below her actual chronological age. The principal therefore suggests that the committee consider retaining Briana (not passing her to the next grade) on that basis. Briana just turned 7, but her age-equivalent language score is 6.0. How would you explain the meaning of an age-equivalent score to the principal and

TABLE 3.1. Test Scores for an Adolescent

Type of test/subtest or area of functioning	Type of score	Score
Intelligence—verbal	Standard score	115
Intelligence—nonverbal	Standard score	103
Reading—reading individual words aloud	Subtest scaled score	8
Reading—answering comprehension questions	Subtest scaled score	11
Math—performing calculations	Subtest scaled score	5
Math—application/word problems	Subtest scaled score	7
Parent-report of attention problems	T-score	62
Parent-report of hyperactivity	T-score	48
Parent-report of anxiety	T-score	73
Parent-report of depression	T-score	65
Parent-report of conduct problems	T-score	34

advise the committee regarding its limitations? What score(s) would you suggest focusing on instead?

3. Robert is a 20-year-old man who recently transferred to Farmland State University after finishing 2 years at Polk County Community College, where his grades were mostly Cs with a few Bs. He has now been experiencing trouble at Farmland State on his exams, and he is actually in danger of failing some of his classes. A psychoeducational evaluation finds that his reading comprehension standard score is 87, based on norms from college juniors nationally. What might be going on here?

4. Jane is a 25-year-old woman who has sought counseling services because she is still quite upset about a romantic break-up that occurred a few months ago. She and her ex-girlfriend had been together for several months, and she is hoping that counseling will help her to move on from that relationship. The counselor, Marla, gives a lengthy trauma symptoms rating scale to all of her clients. The scale has eight subscales, each of which is for a different cluster of trauma symptoms and each of which yields a T-score where higher scores indicate more symptoms and where the cutoff for "clinically significant symptoms" is $T = 65$. Jane's T-scores are under 60 on seven of the eight subscales, but her score on the remaining subscale is 68. Marla concludes tentatively that Jane is suffering from clinically significant trauma-related symptoms. Why is this conclusion premature, and if you were supervising Marla, what advice would you give her, both in completing this evaluation and for future evaluations?

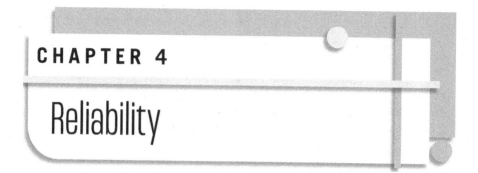

CHAPTER 4

Reliability

Defining Reliability

In everyday conversation, the word *reliable* generally means *dependable* or *consistent*, and in psychometrics, it means roughly the same thing. A reliable car can be counted on to perform under different conditions and over time, and so can a reliable test. This chapter explores in detail how test users can determine how reliable a test is.

Reliability is a concept closely connected to measurement error. All tests are prone to some degree of error; no test is perfectly consistent each time that it is given. Therefore, when someone receives a score on a test, this *observed score* is made up of two components: a *true score* and an *error* value. This is shown in the equation

$$X = T + E$$

where X is the observed score, T is the true score, and E is the error value. (Here, T does not refer to the T-scores from Chapter 3.)

This is all a bit abstract, so to take a concrete example: Jane takes a 10-item multiple-choice science test. She knows eight of the answers, and so in a sense, her "true" score is 8, but she guesses correctly on one of the other two items, and so she receives an observed score of 9. The error is 1. To fill in our equation:

$$X = T + E$$
$$9 = 8 + 1$$

Let's say that Tom takes the same test, and he also knows eight of the answers. But on one of those eight, he carelessly circles the wrong answer. This accident causes him to receive a raw score of 7 on the test. In our equation:

$$X = T + E$$
$$7 = 8 + (-1)$$

Error, then, can either raise or lower the person's true score.

Jane and Tom's test scores are different but not for the right reason—not because they have different levels of science knowledge. Instead, their scores vary because of error caused by transient, random factors. If we had tested them on a different day, Jane might have made a different and incorrect guess, and Tom might have been more careful when circling answers, and their scores would have changed. Guessing and careless mistakes are just two of the many sources of error in test scores. Sometimes students cheat on exams, or there's a loud lawn mower outside the classroom windows that distracts some students more than others. When test scores vary because of these sorts of transient factors, the test's reliability is reduced.

Formally, reliability is often defined as the proportion of variability in the observed scores that is due to variability in true scores:

$$\text{Reliability} = \frac{\text{Variability}_T}{\text{Variability}_X}$$

We want students' test scores to vary based on true, genuine variability in the level of their knowledge, skills, or other traits that the test is designed to measure. In a perfectly reliable test, *all* of the variability in observed scores would come from variability in true scores. Unfortunately, no test in the real world is perfectly reliable. In practice, variability in observed scores comes from (1) variability in true scores *and* (2) sources of measurement error like the ones that we just discussed. Therefore, variability$_T$ will be only one component of variability$_X$, and variability$_X$ will always be greater than variability$_T$.

To better understand this formal definition of reliability, say that we give a 40-item spelling test to a group of six students. It will be easy to find out the students' observed (X) scores—they're whatever scores the students actually got on the test. Now let's pretend that we were able to investigate and find out each student's true score as well. In total, the test score data might look something like Table 4.1. Note that the students' true scores vary—that is, they actually differ in their knowledge of spelling words. However, their T and X scores show some discrepancies, so additional factors besides the true score variability are at work in producing variability in the observed scores. In fact, when we calculate the variance statistic (see Chapter 2) for each of the columns, and we compare the variance in the true scores (25.9) to the variance in the observed scores (31.7), we get a reliability value of (25.9/31.7) = 0.82. Therefore, approximately 82% of the variation in students' (observed) test scores comes from variation in their true levels of spelling knowledge.

Evaluating a Test's Reliability: Background

The example above should help to illustrate the formal definition of reliability. But unfortunately, in the real world we almost never know students' T-values. We can ask if a student guessed, and we can even try to find out if they cheated, but they might not tell the truth, and we'll never really know the precise degree to which they were affected by the noise of a nearby lawn mower. So sadly, we won't be able to calculate reliability in the way that I just did in that example. Thankfully, we don't need to know students' T-values. Psychometricians long ago discovered another formula for reliability: the correlation between observed scores on two *parallel tests*. Parallel tests are defined as a set of two tests in which any specific person would have the

TABLE 4.1. True and Observed Scores for Six Students

Student	T	X
A	27	26
B	23	24
C	34	37
D	31	33
E	39	40
F	29	32

same true score on both tests and in which the two tests show the same variability in observed score values. So to continue with our example of a 40-item spelling test, we could make a *second*, parallel spelling test, also with 40 items. We could have a group of students take both tests, and the correlation between the two sets of observed test scores would be an estimate of (both) tests' reliability values. Consider the two sets of scores shown in Table 4.2 and presented graphically in Figure 4.1. The correlation between these two variables is $r = .78$, and if the two tests were parallel, this would be a good estimate of the tests' reliability. This technique is far more convenient

TABLE 4.2.	Six Students' Scores on Two Parallel Tests of Spelling Skills	
Student	First spelling test X-values	Second spelling test X-values
A	26	24
B	24	31
C	37	35
D	33	31
E	40	37
F	32	34

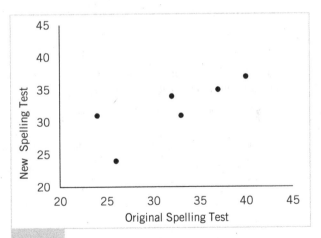

FIGURE 4.1. Scatterplot showing six students' scores on two spelling tests.

than trying to figure out students' individual *T*-values! But where can we find two parallel tests? There are several practical methods for determining a test's reliability that rely on pairs of tests that are *approximately* parallel tests. Each method accounts for a different source of measurement error, as shown in Table 4.3. I now review each method in detail.

Practical Ways of Estimating Reliability

Alternate Form Reliability

Sometimes test designers make multiple separate, complete versions of a test. Classroom teachers don't do this too often at the K–12 level, although college professors sometimes do it to deter cheating. Standardized, high-stakes tests typically have multiple versions; for instance, the SAT that is given in September has different items than the SAT that is given in December. Some diagnostic tests have multiple versions as well; for instance, the Nelson–Denny Reading Test currently has two forms (I and J), whereas the current Woodcock–Johnson Tests of Achievement battery comes in three forms (A, B, and C). When multiple forms of a test are available, whether in a classroom or standardized testing situation, the test versions are known as *alternate forms*, and the correlation between them is known as **alternate form reliability**. The correlation between two forms of a test (Form A and Form B) would look, graphically, something like the scatterplot shown in Figure 4.2 (made with hypothetical data).

TABLE 4.3.	**Various Types of Reliability Coefficients and Sources of Measurement Error They Account For**
Reliability coefficient	**Source of measurement error accounted for**
Alternate form	Variability in the form of test an examiner happens to choose when evaluating an individual; includes factors such as item differences across forms
Internal consistency	Variability in the items chosen for the test, due to imperfect sampling of the domain related to the construct
Test–retest	Variability in the individual's mental state and environment over time
Interscorer	Variability in who is scoring the examinee's responses, including scorers with different biases or levels of competence

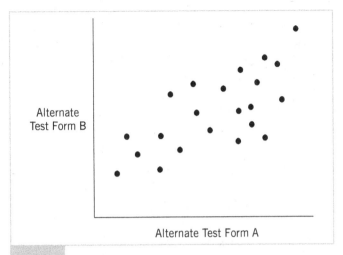

Alternate
Test Form B

Alternate Test Form A

FIGURE 4.2. Scatterplot showing the relationship between a group of students' performance on two alternate forms of a test.

To consider an example from a real test, for 10th graders who took both Forms I and J of the Nelson–Denny Reading Test's vocabulary subtest, the alternate form reliability was .88; that was the correlation between their scores on the two test forms (Fishco, 2019, p. 47). That's a high correlation, suggesting that regardless of whether a student was given Form I or Form J, their score would likely be quite similar.

This approach to estimating reliability has a particular simplicity to it: when constructed properly, alternate test forms do come close to parallel tests. Moreover, when you have multiple versions of a test, you can give them to the same student or group of students to determine the effects of instruction or intervention, and you don't need to worry much about strong practice effects (which might occur if they answered the same items multiple times). Unfortunately, alternate forms have a big disadvantage. In short, making good tests takes a great deal of time and effort, and making *two* good tests takes a lot more resources than making *one* good test, especially when the two tests need to be parallel (or close to it). That's why teachers don't like to make alternate forms of a test; if a student needs a "make-up exam" due to being absent, most teachers are not eager to write an alternate form. A teacher would not only need to think up many more test items but would need to try to make the difficulty roughly the same as the test that the rest of the class took. Many diagnostic tests lack alternate forms for similar reasons; it costs many thousands of dollars to develop a diagnostic test, and it takes even more money to make alternate forms of such a test.

Internal Consistency Reliability

If the elementary school teacher who devised the 40-item spelling test doesn't want to make a second test with another 40 items, what can be done to estimate reliability? One quick solution would be to break the test in half, hoping that the two halves are roughly parallel tests, and then correlating students' scores on the two half tests, as shown in Figure 4.3. We would then have two miniature tests with 20 items each.

This may seem too easy, but in fact reliability estimates based on **split-half** procedures are quite common, given their convenience. However, a simple split-half procedure as just described has two limitations. One limitation is fairly obvious: it's not clear exactly how to split the test in half. If our test has 40 items, how do we get the two sets of 20 items? We could correlate the students' performance on the first half of the test (the first 20 items) with their performance on the second half (the second 20 items), but over the course of the exam, students might get more fatigued, and on many diagnostic tests, the items get harder as they continue, so the two halves

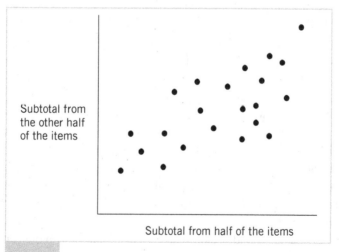

Subtotal from the other half of the items

Subtotal from half of the items

FIGURE 4.3. Scatterplot showing the relationship between a group of students' performance on two halves of a test.

clearly aren't parallel, not even roughly. We could correlate performance on the odd-numbered items (item #1, item #3, item #5, etc.) to performance on the even-numbered items (item #2, item #4, item #6, etc.), but it could still happen, just by chance, that one of those item sets is more difficult than the other. So it seems like the reliability estimate will be heavily dependent on exactly how the test is broken in half.

A second limitation is less obvious: shorter tests tend to be less reliable, and so if we want to estimate the reliability of a 40-item test, and we do this by measuring the correlation between two halves of that test, we'll wind up with an underestimate. Shorter tests with fewer items tend to sample less material, and like small samples of all kinds, smaller samples of test items are more vulnerable to random errors.

Sometimes test developers and researchers compute an odd–even split-half correlation, but more often, they use a statistic called alpha (α) or **Cronbach's alpha** (after the psychologist Lee Cronbach, who developed it). Alpha is a remarkable statistic—it essentially considers all of the possible ways to split your test in half, and it takes the average split-half reliability value from all of those ways, while also adjusting upward to correct for the shortening of the test. It's almost magical how alpha is able to do this, and alpha has become the single most common way to estimate reliability. It is very rare to see a test manual where no alpha statistics are reported.

Alpha and all split-half procedures are referred to as **internal consistency reliability** estimates. They all measure the degree to which different parts of the test are consistent with each other—whether doing well on some of the items on the test is a good gauge of how well people will do on other items in the test. If a test is internally consistent, the relationships between different test parts should be strong. To return to the Nelson–Denny, Cronbach's alpha for the Vocabulary subtest is approximately .93, suggesting that performance on the individual vocabulary items is quite consistent (Fishco, 2019, p. 52).

In recent years, some psychometrics scholars have argued that alpha is not the best measure of a test's internal consistency. These scholars have therefore advocated for other statistics, particularly several versions of a statistic known as *omega* (named after the last letter of the Greek alphabet, just as *alpha* is the first letter). Diagnostic test manuals typically continue to rely on alpha, but if you are reading recent research studies on diagnostic tests, you may come across versions of omega and other measures of internal consistency. In Appendix A, I cite resources on the debate over alpha's utility.

Test–Retest Reliability

Internal consistency reliability is generally a good thing, but it cannot account for error introduced by day-to-day variation in someone's test performance. Part of what we want in a reliable test is one that is reliable over time or *stable*, and to assess this, there's no substitute for actually measuring people twice with a gap in time. When we do this and we correlate the scores from the first test administration with those from the second test administration, we get a **test–retest reliability** estimate. When this is done over long intervals of time, it is sometimes known as a *stability* estimate.

Test–retest reliability is a bit cumbersome to obtain, given the logistical hassles involved in measuring people twice. It is hard enough to get people to show up to a laboratory or clinic even once to take a test battery; it is much harder to get them to come back a second time, particularly when the only purpose is test development and research. For this reason, standardized tests sometimes do not report test–retest reliability at all, and when it is reported, the sample sizes are sometimes quite small. But this type of reliability is often quite valuable and sometimes even more valuable than internal consistency.

You may be wondering about a problem alluded to earlier: practice effects. What if we give students a reading comprehension test twice, keeping the passages and questions the same? Won't students do better the second time, just due to increased familiarity with the materials? Quite possibly. However, if all students experience roughly the same gain, then the correlation between the two test administrations will not be affected. (Correlations do not take into account how close the score values are in an absolute sense; if each student's score went up exactly the same amount on the second administration, the correlation between the scores from the two test administrations would be a perfect positive 1.0.) A related concern is sometimes voiced for personality tests—the concern that on a self-report measure of personality, someone will remember how they answered the last time and give the same answers artificially, just to be consistent. For this reason, for test–retest reliability studies of personality measures, researchers sometimes rearrange the order of the items the second time. In the Nelson–Denny manual, the test–retest reliability coefficient of its Vocabulary subtest is about .96 for high school students, which is very high, although the test–retest interval was only about 2 weeks on average (Fishco, 2019), which is quite small (an issue I return to later in this chapter).

Interscorer Reliability

I haven't yet mentioned a final source of error in test scores: subjectivity in scoring the test items. I always think about this error when I watch an ice-skating competition. Each contestant is scored by several judges, and the judges rarely all agree in their scores. It might be our inclination as viewers to criticize the judges, but some subjectivity is inherent to the task (the ice skating "test"), and if the task can't be scored in a reasonably reliable fash-ion, that's not the judges' fault. The same is true, for instance, when scoring the quality of written essays. Consider, for instance, the essay questions on an Advanced Placement (AP) psychology test. If each essay is only read by a single scorer; would it matter which scorer you get? Or on an IQ test, where a child needs to give narrative definitions for vocabulary words, would it matter which psychologist rates the child's definitions for accuracy? Perhaps of even more concern, we could consider personality judgments made on the basis of therapy clients' responses to inkblot drawings; would two psychologists agree as to the interpretation of those responses?

We address this type of error through measures of **interscorer** (or *inter-rater*) **reliability**. We could ask two English teachers to each score 50 essays on a scale from 1 (very bad) to 10 (excellent), and then we could correlate the two sets of ratings to see how closely the teachers agree. This type of reliability should be measured whenever there is an element of subjectivity in scoring. Writing tasks obviously raise this concern, and so do the verbal parts of many individually administered IQ tests (where students or clients give narrative responses rather than selecting their answers from a small set of options). Also, tasks that require the scorer's very careful attention may raise concerns of scorer error. Such tasks include use of a classroom obser-vation scale for measuring hyperactivity in children, where the scorer must watch a child carefully and rate the child's degree of hyperactivity.

Interscorer reliability is often measured using correlation coefficients, just as the other types of reliability are. However, the typical correlation coefficient that we have been working with (the Pearson correlation coef-ficient, r) is not optimal for measuring agreement between two scorers. A Pearson coefficient only tells us whether two variables are related to each other. To return to an example from above, if we asked two English teachers to score 50 essays, calculating r could tell us whether two teachers both give out higher scores to the same essays. But say that one of the teachers was just a more lenient grader and each of that teacher's ratings was exactly 1 point higher than the other teacher's rating of the same essay. In this case, the *r*-value would be 1.0—there would be a perfect Pearson correlation—because each teacher would rank the essays in the same order. But technically speaking, the teachers didn't actually *agree* on any of their scores; none of the essays received the same score from both teachers. To measure agreement, special types of correlation coefficients known as *intraclass correlation coefficients* (ICCs) can be used, and test manuals will sometimes list ICC values when appropriate. At other times, statistics other than correlation coefficients are used, particularly when judgments are binary (such as pass/fail or present/absent). Imagine that a classroom observation system includes a rating of whether a child is out of their seat during the observation. Rather than a score, each judge will simply conclude "yes" or "no." For data like these, interscorer reliability is often measured using a statistic such as **percent agreement**. You might find that of the 50 judgments each scorer made, they agreed on 45 of them. This would lead to a percent agreement of 45/50 = 90%. A related statistic for binary judgments is kappa (κ), also known as **Cohen's kappa**, after Jacob Cohen, the psychologist who developed it.[1] With these statistics, as is true of a correlation, higher values indicate a more reliable assessment tool.

Interpreting and Applying Reliability Estimates

How High Should Reliability Be?

All other things being equal, higher reliability values are generally better for test quality. Higher values mean that more of the variation in examinees' test scores is due to actual variation in their traits rather than to random noise. Therefore, when choosing between two tests, choosing the one with higher reliability is typically a good idea, if the tests are otherwise

---

[1] Kappa has a notable advantage over percent agreement. Percent agreement is strongly influenced by "chance agreement." Even if two judges are both responding randomly, at times they will agree just by coincidence. Kappa accounts for this by determining how much the judges agreed *beyond what would be expected by chance.* However, in diagnostic contexts, kappa values are influenced by a variety of factors, including whether the condition being diagnosed is common or rare. Therefore, percent agreement has a more intuitive interpretation; you must simply keep in mind that some level of agreement is to be expected even when it is just due to random chance.

comparable. Reliability coefficients generally vary between 0 and 1, and coefficients closer to 1 are generally desirable. But it's not quite that simple in practice; exactly how high the reliability estimate should be depends on what the test is being used for and even on what trait(s) the test is measuring.

As I noted, on standardized tests (including diagnostic tests), the most common statistic reported is alpha, and more generally, internal consistency measures are the most common reliability estimates reported. For these types of estimates, an optimal reliability coefficient is .9 or above. This is sometimes designated "excellent reliability" and can support the use of important decisions regarding individual students or clients (decisions such as clinical diagnosis, special education identification, admission to college, and placement in remedial classes). A reliability coefficient between .8 and .9 is often designated "good reliability," and a test with that reliability can be used as one piece of data, among others, when making a decision, or it can be used to determine if further evaluation is warranted. Finally, reliability coefficients between .7 and .8 are sometimes described as having "adequate reliability" or as being sufficient in the context of research. These standards work reasonably well for alternate-form reliability coefficients and even for interscorer reliability—at least when correlation coefficients are used for the latter. For kappa, these standards are too stringent; because of the way that this statistic is calculated, it is very difficult to get extremely high kappa statistics, and so you can forgive somewhat lower values.

For test–retest reliability coefficients, what's more impressive is that a certain correlation coefficient is found over a longer time interval. Hunsley and Mash (2008) suggested that "excellent" test–retest reliability would be a correlation of .7 or above, when the test–retest interval is at least a year, whereas the same correlation over the course of several months would be "good," and the same correlation over days or weeks would be "adequate."

There's an important caveat to the guidelines that have been given. The type and level of reliability you should demand depend on the trait or skill being measured. For instance, a questionnaire measuring emotional mood would *not* be expected to exhibit high test–retest reliability; part of the nature of moods is that they are expected to change over time, and if a questionnaire shows that different people's moods changed in different directions over time, it does not make the questionnaire bad. A counselor might use a mood assessment at the beginning of his counseling sessions to see what emotional state his clients are in at the moment, without assuming that the emotional state will be stable over time. Even internal consistency reliability estimates assume that different parts of a test should correlate with each other, but occasionally a test measures a set of widely varying skills, making that assumption flawed. In cases like these, certain types of low reliability might not be troublesome. The lesson here is not that you should ignore low reliability estimates but that you should think carefully about what the estimates mean in the context of any particular assessment process.

Factors Affecting Reliability Estimates

We have already alluded to a major factor influencing reliability calculations: the length of a test. Generally, longer tests are more reliable; they give the examinee more opportunities to show their true levels of skills and traits, and they also allow error to average out across more items. This presents a bit of difficulty for the practical evaluator: we want our testing not only to be efficient but also reliable. We often have to compromise one goal to attain the other. Brief questionnaires and short quizzes can be useful, but they should either be used frequently over time with the same examinee or else be used to determine if a more thorough assessment is needed, since they tend to lack high reliability.

Of course, length is a relative term, and the reliability values for any particular measure should always be inspected rather than making assumptions. At times, brief measures are still quite reliable. For instance, the Enculturation Scale for Filipino Americans (ESFA; del Prado & Church, 2010) was developed to measure the degree to which Filipino Americans identified with their Filipino heritage; this is a useful construct to examine in counseling and related contexts. The ESFA was developed in multiple forms, including a long 73-item form and a 30-item short form. The total score for the 73-item version was found to have an internal consistency reliability value of alpha = .89, whereas the 30-item short form generated a total score with alpha = .86. Although reliability dipped slightly, and the ESFA authors do recommend using the longer form, in some situations a small sacrifice in reliability may be worth the significant time savings. In any case, always check the reliability values of available measures to see what your options are.

Length has yet another implication for reliability: Subtests—the individual tasks on a diagnostic test—tend to have lower reliability than overall or composite scores that are formed from the sum or average of several subtests. Therefore, when interpreting an IQ test, the overall or Full Scale IQ tends to be most reliable; the composites for different domains of cognitive ability are somewhat less reliable, and the individual subtest scores are least reliable.[2] For instance, in the fifth edition of the Wechsler Intelligence Scale for Children (WISC-V), the overall, Full Scale IQ has a median internal consistency of .96, whereas the composite for Visual–Spatial Ability (one area of intelligence) has a median internal consistency of .92, and the Block Design subtest (one task that contributes to the Visual–Spatial composite) has a median internal consistency of .84 (Wechsler, 2014, p. 57). These patterns have led some scholars to argue that composite scores should be emphasized when interpreting tests. Certainly, the higher reliability of these scores is a major advantage, but other scholars argue that composites mask variability among the tasks making up each composite. (Of course, if that variability isn't reliable, it's worth masking!)

Since reliability coefficients are (usually) correlation coefficients, they're also affected by factors influencing any correlation coefficient (see the discussion in Chapter 2). For instance, a restricted range will lower reliability; tests that do not generate much variability in scores will not appear to be very reliable. This factor is important to consider when reviewing independent research studies on test reliability; often, researchers use a narrow sample of convenience, such as preschoolers at a Head Start program or students at a top college—samples that might be quite skewed in terms of their members' levels of a trait or skill. These samples will lead to underestimates of the measures' true reliability.

A final factor that can affect reliability is the nature of the sample that is taking the test. Reliability estimates always come from a specific sample; in the case of a diagnostic test, that sample is typically the norm group. If you are administering the test to examinees who differ markedly from the norm group, the reliability estimates in the test manual may not apply, and you may wish to locate independent research studies that were published

---

[2] For this reason, psychometric purists often say that a test does not have a single reliability value; each score from the test has a different reliability value, and even those values will change from one sample to another.

after the test was released, using samples similar to the examinees you are testing.

Applying Reliability Estimates to Individual Scores

A general relationship exists between reliability and the amount of variability in test scores that comes from genuine differences in the level of a trait or skill. If almost all of the variance in observed test scores comes from variability in true scores, the test is very reliable. Unfortunately, a reliability coefficient cannot tell us what an individual examinee's true score is or exactly how much error is in that score. However, the coefficient *does* let us know how confident we can be that the examinee's true score is within a certain distance of their observed score.

To use the reliability coefficient in this way, we compute another statistic, the **standard error of measurement** (SEM), whose formula is

$$SEM = SD_X \sqrt{1 - \text{reliability}}$$

where SD_X is the standard deviation of the observed test scores and "reliability" can refer to any of the types of estimates (e.g., internal consistency, test–retest) discussed earlier. You can think of the SEM this way: due to imperfect reliability, examinees rarely obtain an observed score X that is identical to their true score T. Instead, random error leads to a distribution of X scores surrounding T. The more error that there is (and the lower the reliability), the larger and more spread out the distribution of X scores is. It's similar to when an archer tries to hit a bull's-eye with an arrow: The center of the bull's-eye is where the true score is, but error will lead to a cluster of hits around the center; the archer is unlikely to hit the center each time. Archers with more skill (less error) will have a small cluster around the center; less skilled (less reliable) archers will have a wider cluster. The SEM is the standard deviation of the distribution of X scores surrounding T; it's a measure of how likely X will be far away from T. Higher SEMs mean that examinees' obtained test scores will more likely be farther away from their true scores. SEMs and reliability estimates have a reciprocal relationship; the higher the reliability, the smaller the SEM, and vice versa.

Consider an IQ test in which the standard deviation of the test scores is 15. If the reliability of the Full Scale (overall) IQ score from that test is .95 and a student's true IQ is 110, it's very likely that the student will get a score (an obtained IQ score X) that is pretty close to 110. If the reliability is lower—something like .80—then it's more likely that the same student will obtain an X score farther away from 110. *How* likely? The SEM is key to answering that question.

If the distribution of the X scores around the true score is a normal distribution and the SEM is the standard deviation of that distribution, then we can use the empirical rule (from Chapter 2) to construct confidence intervals around T. About 68% of the X scores will fall within 1 SEM of T; about 95% of the X scores will fall within 2 SEMs of T; and 99.7% of the X scores will fall within 3 SEMs of T. Since in a real-world testing situation, you only have access to X, you can use the process to estimate where T is likely to be.

Let's take the Full Scale IQ with a reliability of .95. The SEM is

$$SEM = SD_X \sqrt{1 - \text{reliability}}$$
$$SEM = 15\sqrt{1 - .95}$$
$$SEM = 15\sqrt{.05}$$
$$SEM = (15)(.2236)$$
$$SEM \approx 3.4$$

As noted, the SEM is approximately 3.4. Say that someone obtains an IQ score of X = 96. We can be 68% confident that the true score will be within 3.4 points of 96—that is, within the interval of 96 ± 3.4, or between 92.6 and 99.4. We can be 95% confident that the true score will be within 6.8 points of 96—that is, between 89.2 and 102.8. And we can be almost certain (99.7% confident) that the true score is within 10.2 points of 96— that is, between 85.8 and 106.2. As you can see, to be more confident, you need to widen the confidence intervals.[3] Figure 4.4 shows the intervals visually as **confidence bands**.

When scores from a standardized test like the SAT are shown visually on a score report, they're often shown within a confidence band that takes imperfect measurement reliability into account. Similarly, when scores from a diagnostic test are reported, they are sometimes given alongside a confidence interval. That kind of presentation helps a wide variety of readers

---

[3] It is rarely necessary to be 99.7%—or even 95%—confident of the score range. Typically, we settle for a 90% confidence interval, which is $X \pm 1.645$ SEM units.

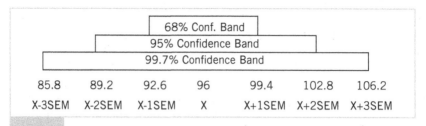

FIGURE 4.4. Confidence bands for an IQ score of 96 from a test with a reliability coefficient of .95.

(students, clients, parents, teachers, etc.) to understand that the examinee's true score is likely to be somewhere within an interval but not necessarily exactly where the observed score is. This also keeps readers from overinterpreting small differences between scores, a topic that I turn to next.

The Implications of Imperfect Reliability

Say that Sally takes a diagnostic reading test that examines her decoding skills (defined as her ability to read increasingly difficult worlds aloud) and her comprehension skills (defined as her ability to correctly answer multiple-choice questions about silently read passages). She obtains the following standard scores:

$$\text{Decoding} = 95$$
$$\text{Comprehension} = 91$$

The reading specialist may be tempted to conclude that Sally's decoding skills are higher than her comprehension skills. But such a conclusion is likely to be extremely misleading. As you know, such standard scores are both in the average range. Moreover, the confidence intervals for these scores likely overlap substantially. For instance, if the *SEM* for each score is 5 (which would correspond to a reliability value between .85 and .90, which is quite good), the 68% confidence intervals lead to these more appropriate reported scores:

$$\text{Decoding} = 95 \pm 5 = 90 \text{ to } 100$$
$$\text{Comprehension} = 91 \pm 5 = 86 \text{ to } 96$$

And the 95% confidence intervals would overlap even more:

$$\text{Decoding} = 95 \pm 10 = 85 \text{ to } 105$$
$$\text{Comprehension} = 91 \pm 10 = 81 \text{ to } 101$$

Now the two scores don't seem so different, right?

The same is true for comparisons across students. Javier and Mac are two friends in 12th grade, and both of them are taking the SAT as part of college application procedures. The SAT Critical Reading section has a mean of approximately 500 and a standard deviation of approximately 100. The SEM is about 30, according to the test makers. If the two students receive the following scores:

$$\text{Javier: } 670$$
$$\text{Mac: } 650$$

Javier may be tempted to tease Mac about the score difference. But given the SEM, the 68% confidence interval for the scores would be:

$$\text{Javier: } 670 \pm 30 = 640 \text{ to } 700$$
$$\text{Mac: } 650 \pm 30 = 620 \text{ to } 680$$

So even at a 68% confidence level, Mac might well have outscored Javier in terms of their true scores. And at a 95% confidence level, we certainly can't tell who outscored whom:

$$\text{Javier: } 670 \pm 60 = 610 \text{ to } 730$$
$$\text{Mac: } 650 \pm 60 = 590 \text{ to } 710$$

In Chapter 3, you may recall that I discussed narrative descriptors for ranges of test scores (e.g., "average"); another reason why such descriptors are useful is that they take imperfect reliability into account. Sally's decoding and comprehension scores are both average, and this way of describing them keeps us from overinterpreting small differences. Similarly, both Javier and Mac clearly did well on the SAT Critical Reading section; their scores would both be above the average range. Sometimes, due to imperfect reliability, we can't give much more information than these broad, somewhat crude descriptions without a significant loss of confidence. The narrative descriptors do have one related potential downside, however; occasionally, they can exaggerate the difference in meaning between similar scores. If 90 is the lower cutoff for the "average" range on an IQ test, and one student receives an 89 while a second student receives a 91, just looking at the narrative descriptors might make the difference between the two scores seem significant, when in fact the confidence bands for the scores almost certainly overlap. This is why looking at the scores themselves is also helpful. In either case, a practitioner armed with knowledge of psychometrics can help examinees and others to understand when score differences are meaningful and when they likely are not.

Reliability of Differences and Profiles

As we just saw, one implication of imperfect test reliability is that we shouldn't make too much of the small differences between test scores. If the tests were given on a different day, for example, the score difference might evaporate or even reverse in direction. We can actually get more specific about the reliability of differences between test scores. When a student or client takes two tests and obtains a score on each, three factors determine how reliable the score difference is:

1. The reliability of Test 1
2. The reliability of Test 2
3. The correlation between Test 1 and Test 2

The first two factors seem obvious; if you don't have two reliable tests to begin with, how can the difference between the test scores be reliable? The third factor matters in a way that you may not expect: *The higher the correlation between the two tests, the less reliable a difference between them is.* Think of it this way: if two tests correlate strongly, scores from those tests should be close to each other. Therefore, if a particular examinee shows a large gap between their scores on those tests, the gap is likely to be due to random error.

Occasionally, important decisions are made on the basis of a gap between test scores. For instance, in some states, learning disabilities can be identified by calculating a gap between an IQ score and a score on an achievement test (measuring reading, math, or writing). Even if the two tests (the IQ test and the achievement test) are themselves reliable, the difference between their scores is still unlikely to be reliable because the two tests are strongly correlated (intelligence and academic skills are closely related to each other, in a statistical sense). This method of learning disability identification is therefore unreliable (see, e.g., Lovett & Gordon, 2005).

At other times, evaluators might note a score profile, such as better performance on a visual task than on a verbal task. Such profiles also tend to be less reliable, in part again due to the fact that the tests making up the profiles often correlate strongly, and in part because some variability across a set of someone's test scores is actually quite common. Any particular large score gap may seem rare, which can lead an evaluator to think there is something unusual about the examinee, but in fact the gap is likely to be due in part to measurement error.

One final comment—the imperfect reliability of measures also leads to a phenomenon known as **regression to the mean**. Briefly, if an examinee obtains a score that is very high or very low (i.e., a score that is far from the mean or average), the next test score obtained is likely to the closer to the mean. The examinee's performance is said to regress to the mean. An implication is that when we find a gap between an extreme score and one closer to the mean, we are likely to be observing regression effects rather than genuine differences in true scores. Consider a student who takes a diagnostic oral language test that measures expressive language (speech) as well as receptive language (listening skills). If the student's expressive language score is very low (say, at the 2nd percentile), their receptive language is likely to be at least somewhat higher (closer to the mean), just by chance. Perhaps a better way of putting this is that the more extreme score (at the 2nd percentile) is likely to be so far away from the mean due partially to random error. Either way, the gap between the more extreme score and the score closer to the mean is likely unreliable. The less reliable the two measures that make up the gap are, the larger regression effects tend to be.[4]

---

[4]I admit that the term *regression to the mean* is a bit confusing because the term *regression* is also used for statistical analyses using correlations to predict things (as in Chapter 2). This is a different usage of the term, although there are historical reasons why the two usages are related.

Item Response Theory

The reliability information covered so far in this chapter has been based on what psychometricians call **classical test theory** (CTT). This theory starts with the simple assumption that each observed test score has a true score and an error score component ($X = T + E$). CTT dates back over 100 years, and it still forms the basis for most diagnostic tests. However, in the past several decades, an alternative approach to understanding reliability (and many other things) has developed, known as **item response theory** (IRT). IRT uses much more advanced mathematics and statistics than CTT, but test users do not need to actually work through IRT equations. Still, a basic understanding of IRT helps test users to think more clearly about items from all tests and to understand certain special types of test scores that come from tests based on IRT.

IRT is a set of statistical models that allow us to estimate the probability of a particular examinee getting a particular item correct. The probability of a correct answer is based on (1) the examinee's ability level and (2) the properties of the item. For instance, a high-ability student in third grade is likely to correctly solve the math equation $8 + 8 = ?$, whereas a low-ability student in the same grade is less likely to solve it correctly. This shows the influence of ability. The high-ability student is also more likely to solve that equation correctly than the same student is to solve this one correctly: $1,961 \div 53 = ?$. This shows the influence of item characteristics, specifically item difficulty. Another item characteristic that matters is item discrimination, which refers to the size of the gap between the performance of low- and high-ability examinees on the item. Yet another characteristic is the probability that getting an item correct just by guessing; true/false items will have a higher probability than four-option multiple-choice items will.

Once IRT is used to develop a test and the characteristics of each item on the test are well understood, we can estimate an examinee's ability level based not only on how many items the examinee answered correctly, but also on *which items were answered correctly*. For instance, answering a more difficult item correctly suggests a higher ability level than answering an easier item correctly. This can even lead to more efficient tests, where an examinee is given items tailored to their ability level. IRT is therefore used in **computerized adaptive testing**, where a computer program adapts to the examinee's estimated ability level by changing which types of items are given, and the resulting test score is based on which items were given and how the examinee answered them. If you took the Graduate Record Examinations (GRE) as part of a graduate school admissions process, you completed a computerized adaptive test like this, and IRT models were used to estimate your ability level. If you did well on an initial set of items, you were given more difficult items later in the test, and your GRE score was based both on which items were given and how well you answered them. If you and a friend each answered 80% of GRE items correctly, but you were given harder items (based on your performance on an initial section), your score will be higher than your friend's. One common diagnostic test battery that was developed using IRT is the Woodcock–Johnson, currently in its fourth edition (the WJ-IV). The WJ-IV is actually three related batteries, measuring a wide array of cognitive abilities, academic skills, and oral language skills. Because IRT estimates are used to generate WJ-IV scores, a computer program must be used to obtain most of an examinee's scores on the test.

IRT-based models make more statistical assumptions about test data than CTT-based models do. For instance, IRT-based models assume that performance on one item will not correlate with performance on other items among examinees with equal ability levels. These assumptions can limit the applicability of IRT, and test developers must always weigh the advantages of IRT against its disadvantages. When reading diagnostic test manuals, you may see IRT mentioned, and it sometimes goes by the name "modern test theory." One type of IRT model, called the Rasch model, may also be mentioned; that model focuses on just one type of item characteristic, item difficulty.

To connect IRT to this chapter in another way, IRT-based tests have a different approach to estimating reliability. Whereas CTT-based test models yield a single reliability statistic of each type (e.g., internal consistency, test–retest), IRT models generally show that the reliability of test scores differs depending on the ability level of the examinee. Specifically, since the majority of the items on most tests are geared toward medium-ability examinees (since that is where most examinees are, as the normal distribution shows), score reliability is highest for medium-ability examinees. Even when we are using tests based on traditional CTT models, as clinicians we should be more careful about assuming that extremely low or extremely high test scores are precise, particularly at the extremes of the age range for the test. On a test with good reliability statistics, we can typically say with confidence that an examinee's true score was very low or very high, but we cannot be as confident about exactly how low or high the true score is. When fewer items are available to estimate ability at the extremes, the scores at the extremes will contain more random error. As this example shows, the development of IRT has helped test users and test developers to better understand the meaning of data from *all* tests.

Conclusions

In one sense, reliability is a simple concept; the everyday meaning of the word maps onto the psychometric meaning. But interpreting reliability estimates is not straightforward, and as test users, we must work with test scores that have imperfect reliability. Moreover, even fairly high reliability estimates lead to confidence bands around scores that are rather wide, and this should give us some humility in interpreting test data. On a different day, or using a different version of the same test, the examinee's score is likely to have been at least a bit different. To be clear, this does not undermine the use of tests; critics of testing point to imperfect reliability as a fatal flaw, but eliminating standardized measurement procedures leaves us with even less reliable guides. Still, large, life-changing, irreparable decisions should be made based on converging evidence from a number of sources rather than just a single test score.

APPLIED EXERCISES

1. A speech-language pathologist gives Janay a language battery, and Janay's overall standard score is 110. The speech–language pathologist checks Janay's file and finds that her IQ score is 125. The speech-language pathologist wonders whether Janay has a language disorder, due to the gap between the IQ score and the language score. But in fact, why are these score data *not* good evidence for a language disorder?

2. A school counselor is considering a standardized survey measure for assessing adolescents' interests in different career paths. The Thompson Career Inventory (TCI) assesses interests in four different career paths: (1) health-related careers, (2) law-related careers, (3) construction and building careers, and (4) education-related careers. A separate score is then given for each career path area; the higher the score, the stronger the interest in those careers. The TCI technical manual shows that all of the scores' alpha coefficients are between .90 and .95. However, the test–retest reliability coefficients for the

scores, over the course of 1 year, are all below .50. How should the scores from this measure be interpreted? What can be concluded about the reliability of the measure more generally?

3. When the school psychologist at Spruance Elementary School performs evaluations on students, she always asks teachers to complete a rating scale on the students' behavioral and emotional problems. One of the most popular rating scales for this type of evaluation is the Teacher Report Form (TRF; Achenbach & Rescorla, 2001). This measure asks teachers about over 100 behaviors that the child may have engaged in (e.g., crying, bullying others) to generate scores in several areas of behavioral and emotional problems. The TRF manual (Achenbach & Rescorla, 2001, p. 101) shows the following alpha coefficients for different scores:

- Affective (Mood) Problems = .76
- Anxiety Problems = .73
- ADHD Problems = .94
- Aggressive Behavior = .95

The TRF uses T scores[5] (mean of 50, SD of 10), where higher scores mean more problems. Usually, 65 or 70 is considered a cutoff for severe problems. What are the SEMs for the scores mentioned above? If Manny, who is referred for concerns related to anxiety, receives an Anxiety Problems T-score of 62 based on his teacher's ratings, what is the 95% confidence interval for his score? How might a counselor's interpretation of the score of 62 change, with and without the confidence interval?

---

[5]Generally, in this chapter, we have used T to refer to an examinee's true score. However, the more typical meaning is a score from the T-distribution ($M = 50$, $SD = 10$) covered in Chapter 3. In this exercise question, the latter meaning is intended.

CHAPTER 5

Validity

If we say that a claim is valid, we generally mean that it's accurate. We administer tests to be able to make claims about examinees—about their levels of knowledge, skills, psychiatric symptoms, and many other things. **Validity** in assessment occurs when we have good evidence that those claims are true. Like a valid claim, a valid test is accurate and allows you to make claims about people that are correct.

To understand the difference between validity and reliability, a historical example is helpful. In the 1800s, scientists believed that intelligence could be assessed by measuring the size of the human skull. The *reliability* of this technique might be quite high. For instance, the measures may show high test–retest reliability, two judges who use the same tape measure might come up with roughly similar measurements, and the measurement technique might even be internally consistent. After all, length measurements taken of the left and right sides of the skull are likely highly correlated. But does any of that make skull measurements a good technique for assessing intelligence? No. Even if skull measurements are reliable, they lack *validity* as a measure of intelligence. Similarly, test scores may show consistency of all kinds but lead to invalid (inaccurate) claims about examinees.

Tests, Constructs, and Inferences

We often say that a valid test measures what it claims to measure. Therefore, if a test designed to measure receptive language skills is valid, it should actually measure receptive language skills. "Receptive language skills" is an example of a **construct**—an unobservable trait of people that our test is claiming to measure. By examining a student's responses to the items on our test, we can begin to make inferences about their level of that construct. Technically speaking, then, a test is (at best) a valid measure only of certain constructs. To say that a test is valid makes no sense without knowing which construct(s) it is trying to measure.[1] When a test has high reliability, it is clearly measuring *something* well, but without evidence of validity, we do not know what that something is. Validity evidence helps to identify the construct that the test is measuring.

Given this situation, some measurement experts argue that it is not *tests* that are valid or invalid but, rather, specific *inferences* made on the basis of test scores. For an analogy, consider a high-quality bathroom scale. With this device, we can make valid inferences about people's weight but not about their level of extraversion. Often, we are tempted to make a wide variety of inferences based on a test score. Consider, for example, a girl in third grade, Lyanna, who obtains a *T*-score of 75 (99th percentile) on the Inattention subscale from a teacher-report behavior rating scale. A test user might want to make any of the following inferences:

1. Lyanna has ADHD, specifically the inattentive type of the disorder.
2. Lyanna should be placed on medication.
3. Lyanna should be seated close to the teacher during class.
4. Lyanna has high levels of inattention.
5. Lyanna reportedly has high levels of inattention symptoms.

Evidence would be needed to validate any of these inferences—even the final one, which seems so obvious. After all, just because the scale is called "Inattention" doesn't mean that the items actually measure that construct. Some of the other inferences need even more evidence; we would need strong evidence to believe that a teacher report of inattention is sufficient to make a diagnosis of ADHD or to recommend various interventions

---

[1] To return to our historical example, skull measurements may be useful for certain purposes (indeed, archaeologists use them widely today to study human evolution), but they are not valid measures of the construct of intelligence.

and accommodations. The bottom line is that depending on the specific validity evidence, some of the claims could be valid, whereas others are not.

Types of Validity Evidence

It is tempting to casually look at test materials and form a judgment regarding the test's validity. At times, this superficial technique seems to support the test, as in a personality test that claims to measure extraversion and asks people how much they enjoy going to parties. When a test's items seem to relate obviously to the construct of interest, the test is said to have **face validity**. Unfortunately, this casual approach is generally not sufficient to support the claims we wish to make about examinees. However, a wide variety of sources of useful validity evidence is available.

Evidence from Test Content

Consider again that final, humble inference about Lyanna, that based on her high Inattention score on the teacher-report behavior rating scale, we can conclude that her teacher describes her as having high levels of inattention symptoms. It would be helpful to inspect the items on the Inattention subscale of the behavior rating scale to determine if the items actually concern inattention. Psychological research and theory on inattention describes such problems as difficulty concentrating, being easily distracted, and not listening when being spoken to, so we would expect the items to mention these kinds of behaviors. This would be evidence of validity from the content of the test—what is sometimes known as *content validity*. If, despite the subscale's name ("Inattention"), its items did not cover such behaviors and were about issues such as hyperactivity, the validity of our claim regarding Lyanna would be threatened. In a sense, what differentiates content validity from face validity is (1) the judge's level of expertise and (2) the judge's explicit use of scientific work (research and theory) to determine how relevant the item content is to the construct of interest.

Content validity is easiest to measure when we can compare the items on a test to some kind of official list of content that the test is expected to cover. For instance, the official diagnostic criteria for ADHD (found in the fifth edition of the *Diagnostic and Statistical Manual of Mental Disorders* [DSM-5]) list nine official symptoms related to inattention (American

Psychiatric Association, 2013). The Conners Adult ADHD Rating Scale (CAARS; Conners et al., 1999) generates a DSM Inattentive Symptoms score, based on nine items whose language is taken from the DSM—a great piece of evidence for that score's content validity. That kind of evidence could even help to support a claim that someone meets the criteria for a DSM diagnosis of ADHD (although other evidence would also be needed to draw such a conclusion with confidence).

Similarly, on standardized educational tests, there is often a content outline or a set of "specifications" for the test, listing the topics to be covered. Content validity can be evaluated by examining the degree to which the test items match up with the information and skills in the content outline. Consider a test of general biology knowledge whose content outline has five broad areas:

1. Evolutionary theory
2. Cell biology and genetics
3. Plant structure and function
4. Animal structure and function
5. Ecology

These areas are thought to be equally important. If the test has 100 items, we would be disappointed to find that none of the items are devoted to ecology. It would be even worse if several of the items concerned physics—a topic that was nowhere in the content outline. These two scenarios illustrate two threats to content validity: **construct underrepresentation** (failing to measure parts of the construct—here, general biology knowledge) and **construct-irrelevant variance** (measuring things beyond the construct). Students often complain about these problems with teacher-made tests, and sometimes the complaints are well founded. Teachers, including college professors, typically get little training in how to develop assessment tools, and the resulting instruments sometimes do have these content validity problems.

At times the strength of content validity evidence can be quantified. For instance, you can calculate the percent of items on an ADHD rating scale that refer to official DSM symptoms. Alternatively, a test developer can ask experts in a content domain to judge whether each item on a test is part of the core construct being measured and to compute a percentage as well. Some psychometricians have developed more statistically sophisticated strategies for measuring content validity evidence, too (e.g., Sireci, 1998). These strategies sometimes involve asking experts to rate each item's relevance on a quantitative scale, or presenting item pairs and asking experts to rate the similarity of the two items in each pair (in terms of the constructs that the two items seem to measure). When reviewing tests for use in clinical settings, there is no substitute for having clinical professionals carefully inspect the actual test stimuli and items, and comparing those to authoritative or official descriptions of the constructs to be measured. This is certainly not the only type of validity evidence, but content validity is often important in measurement, particularly when defending the relevance of test scores to audiences who may be skeptical.

Convergent and Discriminant Evidence

Another type of validity evidence involves correlating a test with other tests designed to measure the same or similar constructs. The resulting relationships are sometimes described as evidence of **convergent validity**; multiple tests of the same construct should converge on similar scores. If five IQ tests all claim to measure general intelligence, they should yield similar scores on the same child. Therefore, if a new test has been developed to measure math skills, it is often validated by correlating performance on the new measure with performance on an older, established measure of math skills; this leads to a scatterplot such as the one shown in Figure 5.1. The scatterplot shows that generally students with higher scores on the new Thompson measure also get higher scores on the older Johnson measure. Similarly, when a new, updated edition of a test appears, the validation evidence often includes correlating it with the previous edition; after all, the different editions of the test have been designed to measure the same construct. Rarely is a new test the first one of its kind, and so test developers usually have their choice of a number of other measures to use to assess convergent validity.

A related form of convergent validity evidence consists of finding expected group differences on a test. For instance, if a behavior rating scale of ADHD symptoms is valid, students who have a prior, independently established diagnosis of ADHD should receive higher symptom ratings (suggesting worse symptoms) on the scale than a non-ADHD sample does. Finding no group differences would be so odd as to cast doubt on whether

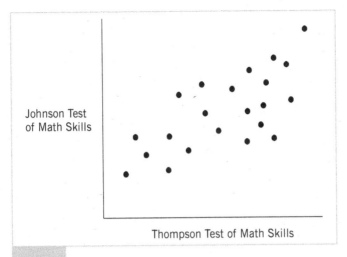

Johnson Test of Math Skills

Thompson Test of Math Skills

FIGURE 5.1. Scatterplot showing the relationship between scores from two hypothetical tests of mathematics skills.

the scale was really measuring ADHD symptoms. Similar analyses are done on measures of cognitive and academic performance. For instance, as the Wechsler Intelligence Scale for Children, Fifth Edition (WISC-V) was being validated, test developers compared children with and without prior diagnoses of intellectual disability—a condition whose hallmarks include low intelligence. Those children with diagnoses of moderate intellectual disability obtained an average Full Scale (total) IQ score of 49.7, much lower than the average IQ (98.5) of a control group (Wechsler, 2014, p. 120). Had this difference not been significant, the validity of the WISC-V would be open to serious question, since children with intellectual disability *should* receive very low scores on a measure of intelligence. The children's prior, independent diagnoses should converge with the results of the WISC-V, demonstrating validity.

Other types of group comparisons can also constitute evidence of validity. For instance, if students with low reading skills are given a reading intervention that prior research has shown to be highly effective, the students' scores on a valid test of reading skills should rise. Researchers can compare students' scores before and after the intervention to help validate the test's ability to detect the effects of the intervention. Similarly, a new measure of depression symptoms should be sensitive to changes in symptoms that clients experience in response to antidepressant medication that is already known to be effective. Finally, changes in scores on some measures are expected based simply on the passage of time; a measure of grip strength should detect age-related increases in average strength as children grow older. All of these types of group comparisons show convergent validity evidence because they find agreement between our measure and other indices of a construct (e.g., experience with effective treatments or expected maturation over time).

A related type of validity evidence shows a *lack of relationship* between a test and measures of theoretically unrelated constructs—we call this **discriminant validity** evidence. In essence, a valid test should be able to discriminate (distinguish) between different constructs, measuring one but not the others. When paired with convergent validity evidence, it can be quite important to know this information. For instance, if we develop a measure of verbal intelligence for preschool children, there may be a concern that shy preschoolers will be unfairly penalized because they are intimidated by the test situation, whereas social, extraverted children will get a boost in scores. If we find that scores on the verbal intelligence test do *not* correlate with ratings of the children's extraversion levels, this would be good discriminant validity evidence; our test is able to discriminate between extraversion and verbal intelligence.

Convergent and discriminant validity evidence work together to help us understand what a test is really measuring. Seeing how a test correlates with many other measures gives us a sense of how it fits in among a network of different constructs. For instance, consider a new reading comprehension test in which a student is asked to read passages silently, and after reading each passage they indicate they are finished, the passage is removed, and they are asked questions about the passage. Doing well on the test might seem to require good memory rather than merely comprehension of the passages. If we correlated scores on this test with (1) other measures of reading comprehension where the passages are available for reference when answering comprehension questions, as well as correlating the test scores with (2) tests designed to measure students' memory skills, we could find whether the new reading comprehension test was more a measure of reading comprehension or memory. If the test is designed to measure reading comprehension rather than memory, we should find convergent validity evidence (strong positive correlations) with other measures of reading comprehension (even those with a somewhat different format), whereas we should find discriminant validity evidence (weak or zero correlations) with measures of memory. If we find similarly strong correlations with both types of measures, we might conclude that the new test measures a composite construct: reading comprehension *and* memory for text.

Test–Criterion Relationships

Some tests are developed mainly to predict outcomes. The clearest examples are tests used in admissions and selection procedures. For instance, the SAT and ACT are used to predict performance in college, and certain employment tests are used to predict job performance. The inferences that are typically made on the basis of examinees' scores on these tests are about the examinees' future performance, and so the most logical way of obtaining validity evidence is to correlate the test scores with that future performance. This is called **predictive validity** evidence—data showing that a test predicts some outcome in the future.

At times, the future outcomes being predicted are negative rather than positive ones; here, prediction is even more important. For instance, determining suicide risk is a high-stakes practice in clinical assessment. The Beck Depression Inventory (BDI) is a popular self-report questionnaire that includes an item asking about suicidal thoughts. The validation evidence for that specific item includes its ability to predict the chances that a client will attempt suicide and die by suicide (e.g., Green et al., 2015). Similarly, in forensic psychological assessment, clinical professionals administer standardized interviews and tests to determine the chance that a criminal will commit another crime. The validation evidence for those assessment tools involves correlations between assessment data and future criminal behavior.

Even when a test has not been designed solely to make predictions, predictive validity evidence can be helpful in showing that a test is measuring the construct it claims to measure. For instance, in psychological theory and research, the construct of intelligence is related to the construct of academic skills; intelligence is understood to be beneficial for acquiring academic skills. Therefore, if a test of intelligence is valid, it should predict future academic achievement. Similarly, a valid measure of early literacy skills (e.g., the ability to name alphabet letters) should predict reading performance at the end of first grade.

Predictive validity evidence is impressive; the idea that a snapshot of behavior at one point in time can effectively predict an important outcome months or years later is a bit stunning when you stop to think about it.

Depending on the strength of the relationships found (an issue that I discuss in more detail below), predictive validity evidence can lead to relatively bold and confident claims about examinees. Unfortunately, such evidence can be logistically difficult to obtain; students or clients need to be followed up over long periods of time, often by researchers who do not have regular access to the examinees (unlike educators and clinicians). Therefore, researchers sometimes collect **concurrent validity** evidence—that is, evidence of relationships between a test and other measures gathered at the same time point (i.e., concurrently). Together, predictive and concurrent validity evidence are both forms of **criterion-related validity** evidence, since both involve correlating test scores with some external criterion.

Criterion-related validity correlations are often interpreted through the coefficient of determination, r^2. You might recall from Chapter 2 that this statistic tells us the percent of variability in an outcome that is accounted for by variability in our test or predictor. If an IQ score obtained at the beginning of the school year predicts students' end-of-grade state reading test score at $r = .50$, the coefficient of determination is $r^2 = .25$, and we can conclude that 25% of the variability in the reading score is accounted for by variability in IQ. Although 25% may seem small, it is actually rather remarkable that we can account for a quarter of variability in performance nearly a year after we give a test, considering all of the other factors that can affect someone's score on the reading test. This would be quite strong predictive validity evidence.

Before moving on, I note a final type of criterion-related validity: **incremental validity**. Very often, test users want to know if a particular test score adds meaningfully to our assessment data. For instance, when making admissions decisions, colleges already have access to applicants' high school grades, and so admissions officers may wish to know if the SAT can help predict students' college performance *over and above the prediction afforded by high school grades*. In a diagnostic context, a counseling center might already have all clients complete a nine-item checklist of the official symptoms of a depressive episode, and so the staff wants to know if adding the Beck Depression Inventory actually adds to the prediction of a particular outcome (such as receiving a formal diagnosis of clinical depression). Incremental validity is especially important if a measure is expensive or logistically intensive.

To determine if incremental validity evidence is present for a measure, researchers use multiple regression (as described in Chapter 2). Typically, a regression analysis is performed where first an already-established assessment tool is used to predict an outcome. Then the new assessment tool is added as a second predictor, and the researchers see if the R^2 for explaining variance in the outcome goes up significantly (and by how much). Alternatively, researchers can simply use both predictors in the regression analysis at the same time and check if the standardized regression (beta) weight for the new proposed measure is statistically significant (and how large the weight is).

Evidence from Internal Structure

Almost all tests are composed of many different items, often organized into subtests. The structure of a test should parallel the structure of the construct that the test is designed to measure. Sometimes the construct is relatively simple—say, spelling skills. The structure of the test could be similarly simple—perhaps just a list of increasingly complex words read aloud, with the student expected to write down the appropriately spelled word. We should expect that such a measure will show high internal consistency reliability (as seen in Chapter 4), and there are more sophisticated statistical analyses that can confirm that the measure, like the skill, is *unidimensional*.

At other times, the construct is complex and *multidimensional*. For instance, spelling skills can be considered a subarea of the construct of academic achievement. That umbrella construct can be divided into the domains of reading, math, and writing skills, and each of those domains has subskills. A full academic achievement test might have six subtests:

1. Reading—decoding (reading individual words aloud)
2. Reading—comprehension (reading passages silently and answering multiple-choice questions about them)
3. Mathematics—computation (solving numerical equations)
4. Mathematics—reasoning (solving word problems)
5. Writing—spelling (writing down dictated words)
6. Writing—composition (writing an essay on a given topic)

The battery might yield six separate scores—one for each subtest—as well as three domain scores (one each for reading, math, and writing), and finally an overall score for academic achievement. The latter score might have only modest internal consistency reliability, since it is made up of items measuring such different skills. However, the structure of the measure (the organization of the six subtests) clearly parallels our understanding of the construct of academic achievement. Moreover, we would expect the six subtests to show expected relationships with each other—for instance, the two reading tests should be more strongly correlated with each other than either is with the math tests. Data on these relationships would also constitute evidence of the test's internal structure.

In essence, we are looking for internal structure data that "make sense," given our prior knowledge about the nature and structure of the construct(s) that the test is designed to measure. Internal structure data are often obtained through a statistical procedure called *factor analysis*. In Chapter 6, I discuss factor analysis in great detail, since it is an important part of psychometrics more generally. For now, I'll just note that when factor analysis data show an internal structure that's expected, given our understanding of the construct to be measured, this is evidence that the test is indeed measuring the intended construct, and so it is evidence of validity.

The Consequences of Test Use

The types of validity evidence that we've reviewed so far—evidence from test content, convergent and discriminant relationships, test-criterion relationships, and internal structure—are all well accepted among measurement experts. Test manuals routinely include these types of evidence. A final type of evidence is more controversial: evidence of the consequences of test use. Some psychometricians argue that if a test shows the traditional types of validity evidence already reviewed, the case for validity is extremely strong, at least for certain inferences about examinees. Other psychometricians argue that an important issue is being neglected: the effects of test use on society, including on the examinees.

To understand this concern, consider the IQ test. IQ tests are generally the "gold standard" when it comes to psychometric quality. They predict a wide variety of external criteria, including in the future (predictive validity), and they are designed to represent many of the areas of cognitive ability that research has identified (content validity). Moreover, they tend to correlate with each other (convergent validity) but not with theoretically unrelated tests (discriminant validity), and their internal structure often mirrors their design. By all of these traditional standards, they are unparalleled. At the

same time, IQ tests are controversial, in large part because their consequences are controversial. For example, IQ tests are often used to identify some students with stigmatizing labels such as intellectual disability
(formerly known as mental retardation), while certifying other students as
being "mentally gifted," a highly desirable designation. The former group
of students is often removed from their peers and placed in special, slower
classes, whereas the latter group is given enjoyable enrichment activities.
Some scholars believe that these placements and education strategies are
justified, whereas others disagree. Critics of IQ tests are unimpressed by
the traditional types of validity evidence, and would be concerned that by
calling the tests "valid," people will assume that the tests are unambiguously
good and used well.

The rationale behind considering what some measurement experts
have called *consequential validity* is understandable. Test use is where psychometrics meets the real world, after all. But counting consequences as
part of validity keeps us from making an objective evaluation of a test's
validity evidence, since different reviewers will disagree on whether the
consequences of test use are good or bad. Social and political values play
a large role in determining our views of the consequences of test use, and
these values prevent a test user (a typical clinician or diagnostician) from
simply looking up an unbiased account of a test's validity evidence in a
reference book. In addition, the consequences of test use may take years or
decades to become apparent, and so test developers cannot wait for such
data before publishing and promoting a test. For these reasons, test manuals rarely discuss the consequences of test use, and it is not clear that those
consequences are actually part of validity evidence. Nonetheless, test users
and policymakers should obviously be alert to consequences and consider
them in designing testing programs. I return to this topic in Chapter 7,
which covers test bias and fairness.

Validity and Classification

Often, we conduct assessments to make binary (yes-or-no) decisions about
diagnosis, identification, qualification, placement, selection, and other functions. Does this child have a speech/language impairment or not? Should
this student be held back or be moved up to third grade? Does this client

meet the clinical criteria for generalized anxiety disorder or not? Many test manuals report validity evidence that applies specifically to these kinds of binary decisions, where we are classifying examinees into two groups. Sometimes this evidence is covered under the heading of "clinical utility."

To understand this kind of evidence, we can consider the four different possible outcomes of a classification decision. I'll phrase these outcomes in terms of (a) whether or not an examinee actually has a "condition" (such as a disorder or disability) and (b) whether or not the test score suggests that the examinee has the condition. The four possible outcomes are these:

1. The examinee tests positive for a condition—that is, the test score suggests that the examinee has the condition—and this classification is correct, since the examinee does in fact have the condition. We call this a **true positive**.

2. The examinee tests negative for a condition, but the classification is incorrect. The examinee actually does have the condition. This is a **false-negative** test result.

3. The examinee tests positive for a condition, but the classification is incorrect. The examinee actually doesn't have the condition. This is a **false-positive** test result.

4. The examinee tests negative for the condition, and the classification is correct, since the examinee doesn't have the condition. This is a **true-negative** test result.

The four outcomes can be arranged as shown in Table 5.1.

TABLE 5.1. **Four Possible Outcomes of Diagnostic Decision Making**		
	Examinee has condition	**Examinee does not have condition**
Test result is positive for condition	True positive— correct decision	False positive— incorrect decision
Test result is negative for condition	False negative— incorrect decision	True negative— incorrect decision

If this terminology sounds like it comes from medical tests, it's exactly the same. "Positive" doesn't mean "good"—it often means that someone has a disorder. To apply this to a concrete situation, say that a standardized parent-report rating scale is being used to identify ADHD in a referred child, an 8-year-old boy named Liam. Perhaps Liam has ADHD, or maybe he doesn't. The evaluator will try to find out by using the rating scale, but the scale isn't perfect, particularly without other evidence. The scale offers a suggested cutoff score—a T-score of 65—to make the binary decision, but there's a chance that the classification decision about Liam might fall into any of the four cells of Table 5.1. If the manual reports validation data showing the chances of each of the four outcomes, this can be of enormous benefit to the clinician. Say that the test developers conducted a validation study where they examined 200 children, 100 of whom had a prior, independent, high-quality diagnosis of ADHD. The other 100 children underwent the same high-quality evaluation procedures, which confirmed that the group did *not* have ADHD. The developers then administered the rating scale to the 200 children's parents to see if the scale would be correct for each child. The study yielded the data shown in Table 5.2.

As you can see, of the 100 children who we know have ADHD, 90 of them (90/100 = 90%) were correctly detected by the rating scale. This is known as the **sensitivity** of the measure; the scale is 90% sensitive (it is sensitive enough to catch 90% of children who have ADHD). Of the 100 children who we know do not have ADHD, 70 were correctly classified. This is the **specificity** of the scale—it is 70% specific, since its positive results are mostly specific or limited to children with ADHD. But 30% of the time that a child doesn't have ADHD, they test positive on the rating scale anyway.

TABLE 5.2. Diagnostic Accuracy of a Hypothetical ADHD Rating Scale	Child has ADHD	Child does not have ADHD
Rating scale $T \geq 65$ (positive test result)	90	30
Rating scale $T < 65$ (negative test result)	10	70

To take another example, let's look at real data from the Nelson–Denny Reading Test (NDRT). The test has an overall score known as the Reading Index, and it's on a standard score scale ($M = 100$, $SD = 15$). The lower the Reading Index, the lower the individual's reading skills are (and the more likely it is that they are impaired in reading). In one validity study, the test developers examined 466 people, half (233) of whom had a prior diagnosis of a learning disability in reading. The developers then looked at the accuracy of a Reading Index cutoff score of 90 in identifying those with and without a diagnosis, yielding the data in Table 5.3 (from Fishco, 2019, p. 76). Of the 233 people with a learning disability in reading, the NDRT Reading Index cutoff caught 161, giving a sensitivity of 161/233, or 69%. Of the 233 people without a diagnosis, the NDRT correctly showed no significant reading problems in 199 of them, giving a specificity of 199/233, or 85%.

Sensitivity and specificity are both desirable qualities in a measure, and higher levels of both lead to better, more accurate classification decisions. Unfortunately, the two are often in tension; the more sensitive a test is, the less specific it will tend to be, and vice versa. To understand why this is the case, say that we want to increase the sensitivity of the rating scale described in the first example. Ninety percent is a good sensitivity value, but there were still 10 children whose ADHD went undetected by the scale. We could lower the T-score cutoff from 65 to 60, in the hopes that some of those 10 children might at least have scored a 60 or higher and will be detected by this lower cutoff. But if we move the cutoff in that direction, we will also be likely to misclassify more children who do not have ADHD, and our false-positive rate may go from 30% to 40% or even higher. You can think of this as a general principle of clinical decision making: the more that you lower your threshold to try to catch every student or client who might need assistance, the more that you will wrongly identify folks who do not actually need assistance. Meanwhile, raising your thresholds to avoid false diagnoses

TABLE 5.3. Diagnostic Accuracy of the NDRT Reading Index

	Has learning disability in reading	No diagnosis
NDRT Reading Index < 90 (test positive for reading problems)	161	34
NDRT Reading Index > 89 (test negative for reading problems)	72	199

will make it more likely that you ignore folks who are in genuine need of identification. Depending on the situation, sensitivity may be more important than specificity or vice versa. For instance, in a screening context—where we are simply trying to determine who needs more comprehensive evaluation—sensitivity is more important. If our screening measure leads to a false positive, it only means that someone gets more assessments, which will presumably show that the person does not actually have the condition in question. In contrast, when we are making a high-stakes clinical decision where a false-positive identification could lead to serious harm (e.g., treatment with a medication that has dangerous side effects), specificity is more important.[2]

Sensitivity and specificity are useful statistics, and other things being equal, you should prefer measures with higher levels of both. However, they both tell us what the chance is of testing positive after we already know the examinee's genuine status. In terms of formal probabilities, sensitivity and specificity describe the probability of (for instance) a positive ADHD test result, *given the examinee's actual ADHD status*. It is even more useful to know the reverse of this probability—to know the probability that the examinee has ADHD, given that they tested positive for it on our measure. This is known as the **positive predictive value** (PPV), and its counterpart is the **negative predictive value** (NPV)—the chance that the examinee does not have ADHD, given that they tested negative.

PPV and NPV are closely related to sensitivity and specificity. All other things being equal, higher sensitivity leads to a higher NPV, since if a test is highly sensitive (i.e., it will detect almost all true cases), then you can be confident that a negative test result means that the person does not have the condition (high NPV). Similarly, a higher specificity tends to lead to a higher PPV, since in a highly specific test (one that only shows a positive result if someone has the condition), you can be more confident that

---

[2] In many cases, sensitivity and specificity are both very important. (Another way to think about this is that in many cases, false positives and false negatives can both be very bad.) For this reason, there is a statistic called *classification accuracy* that combines both sensitivity and specificity. This statistic answers the following question: Of all of the participants in the classification study, what proportion of the classifications were correct? In our ADHD example, out of the 200 children studied, 160 (90 + 70) were classified correctly, and so the classification accuracy is 160/200 = 80%. In the NDRT data, of 466 people, 360 (161 + 199) were classified correctly, and so the classification accuracy is 360/466 = 77%.

positive test results are accurate (high PPV). However, the PPV and NPV also depend on the general prevalence of a condition (this is known as the condition's **base rate**). Tests for high-prevalence (common) conditions will have higher PPVs and lower NPVs, since it is always more likely that an examinee has a common condition than a rare one.

The effect of a base rate on PPV and NPV values is enormous. Consider a hypothetical test designed to classify neurological patients as having expressive aphasia (a language disorder involving difficulties with articulate speech). Imagine that the sensitivity of the test is .80 (i.e., 80% of individuals with independent diagnoses of expressive aphasia will be classified as such by the test), while the specificity is .95 (i.e., 95% of those patients who do not have expressive aphasia will be classified by the test as not having the disorder). Now, take an individual who "tests positive" for expressive aphasia on the test; what is the chance that the person actually has the disorder? If the base rate of expressive aphasia in the testing setting is 50%, as might be the case in a neurological rehabilitation facility, the PPV will be 94.1%, which is excellent; you can be almost certain that the person who tests positive actually has the disorder. If the base rate is 5%, as might be the case in an outpatient neuropsychology practice, the PPV drops to only 46%. A positive test result in the outpatient practice setting will only indicate expressive aphasia 46% of the time, although this is still far above the base rate of 5% in that setting (all numbers are taken from Bennett et al., 1998). Therefore, when test manuals give PPV and NPV statistics, the manuals must specify a particular base rate prevalence level (usually based on prior research or official epidemiology statistics). Moreover, if you are working in a setting or location where you know that there is a higher or lower prevalence of the condition, you should adjust your interpretation of the values accordingly.

Evaluating Validity Evidence

In Chapter 4, we saw that evaluating reliability evidence can be a bit complicated. If anything, evaluating validity evidence is even *more* complicated. With regard to reliability, we're just trying to get a sense of an examinee's true score. With regard to validity, we're trying to figure out what construct the true score is an index of and to find evidence justifying any of a wide variety of inferences about the examinee. Depending on the claims we want to make, there is different validity evidence to seek.

Validity of Different Inferences

Sometimes we are simply interested in inferring the examinee's level of some skill or trait—the construct to be measured. For instance, some school psychologists include an IQ test in virtually all evaluation batteries for students doing poorly in school. The purpose of the test is to get a sense of the student's overall cognitive ability to determine if low ability may explain the poor school performance. For such a purpose, the validity evidence to be sought is usually for the overall composite (Full Scale) IQ score, and the evidence consists of all the data suggesting that the score measures intelligence. This data might include content validity evidence showing that the tasks on the IQ test cover many different areas of cognitive ability, criterion-related validity evidence showing that the IQ score correlates with things that intelligence should correlate with; and evidence showing an internal structure for the test that roughly mirrors what research has shown the structure of intelligence to be.

At other times, we are interested in using a measure to identify a clinical disorder or disability condition. For instance, a counselor might be considering a diagnosis of generalized anxiety disorder (GAD), in part on the basis of data obtained from a self-report symptom rating scale. The scale gives a guideline that raw scores over 20 are suggestive of clinically significant anxiety. The relevant validity evidence might include group comparisons of individuals with and without independent diagnoses of GAD—particularly if the evidence shows that the vast majority of those with untreated GAD score over 20 (i.e., high sensitivity). Convergent validity evidence showing correlations between this rating scale and older, lengthier, established scales would also be helpful. If the counselor is interested in differentiating between GAD and depression in a particular client (a differentiation that can be difficult to make based solely on the initial referral complaints), the counselor might seek discriminant validity evidence showing that the rating scale has no more than a weak relationship with measures of depression.

At other times, test users may be seeking one specific type of validity evidence. For instance, before using an IQ test as part of a gifted identification process, evidence that the IQ test predicts future educational performance would be helpful. Similarly, if a school-based speech-language pathologist uses a teacher-report rating scale to screen students for auditory processing disorder and plans to refer any students with a positive test result for a full evaluation by an audiologist, evidence of the rating scale's very high sensitivity to auditory processing disorder would be very important, but specificity would not be as important.

There is a special issue to note for tests that generate many distinct test scores: validity evidence should be present for any scores that are interpreted and used. For instance, as mentioned earlier, a diagnostic battery of academic skills may generate an overall academic skills score, separate domain scores for reading, math, and writing, and scores for individual subtests measuring decoding, math reasoning, and so on. When assessing a student for a learning disability, if the identification criteria require poor performance at the level of a whole academic skill domain (e.g., reading), the domain scores should have validity evidence. If instead a student can be identified based on a single subtest score, each of those scores should also have validity evidence. Often, just as with reliability, the validity evidence for subtest scores is weaker than that of composite scores; as such, composite scores should generally be weighted more in decision making.

Regardless of the purpose of the test use, I recommend reading the validity section of a test manual completely to learn the totality of the validity evidence that was present at the time the test was published. Often, as test users, we are not able to think about all of the evidence that might be relevant to our test use. It's better to let the test developers present their case for the validity of the measure and consider, while reading, whether the evidence presented in the manual provides sufficient justification for what we're planning to do with the measure. If the justification is not clear, consider looking up additional research that has been done with the measure after it was published. Test developers cannot wait several years to conduct lengthy validity studies before publishing a test. Moreover, much of the important validity evidence may only accumulate after publication—meaning that the evidence will not be in the manual. Updated professional textbooks and review articles in professional journals are also often available to summarize the post-publication validity studies on different measures.

Interpreting the Strength of Validity Evidence

As we have seen, some validity evidence comes in the form of correlations between a test and other measures. The resulting correlation data are called **validity coefficients.** In our discussion of reliability coefficients in Chapter 4, we provided rough guidelines that described what "good" or "excellent" reliability coefficients look like. In the case of validity, it is more difficult to give broadly applicable guidance, since what counts as good validity evidence will depend on the specific interpretations and uses of test scores, and some important validity evidence will not come in the form of correlation coefficients. With those caveats, here are several rules of thumb to keep in mind when reviewing validity evidence:

1. Convergent validity coefficients between a measure and other measures of the same construct should be positive, statistically significant, and strong, preferably 0.50 or above. The higher they are, the better; it is not unusual to find two IQ tests whose full-scale scores correlate over 0.70, for instance.

2. With test-criterion relationships (i.e., concurrent and predictive validity), again significant positive correlations are expected, with stronger correlations being better. However, these correlations will often be lower than convergent validity coefficients, especially when we are predicting outcomes some distance into the future. Even then, statistically significant relationships are desirable.

3. With discriminant validity, the opposite is true; coefficients closer to zero are better. This is not always reasonable; different constructs in psychology do tend to relate to each other. Sometimes it is more worthwhile to check if the discriminant validity coefficients are simply lower than the convergent validity coefficients. Consider two batteries of language skills, each of which generates two composite scores, one for expressive language (speech) and one for receptive language (listening skills). The correlation between the expressive language composite scores on the two batteries (convergent validity) should be higher than the correlation between the expressive and receptive scores within each battery, if the batteries are truly able to discriminate between expressive and receptive language.

4. When group comparisons are used as validity evidence, larger group differences are generally better. These differences are often presented as group means and standard deviations, and sometimes an effect-size value is given. If not, it is easy to calculate using a web calculator. The effect-size statistic d, sometimes known as the standardized mean difference or Cohen's d (after Jacob Cohen, the same psychologist who developed the

kappa statistic), tells us how many standard deviations apart the groups are, and for many comparisons, we would expect a d of at least 0.50. (Return to Chapter 2 for a more detailed discussion of Cohen's d.)

5. Although statistical methods are available for quantifying the degree of content validity evidence, they are rarely found in test manuals, at least beyond presenting simple percentages. When the construct to be measured has an official set of detailed specifications (e.g., the curriculum to be covered or the diagnostic criteria for a disorder), it is easy for test makers to calculate the degree of overlap between the specifications and the test content. In other cases, evidence will be presented in a qualitative form.

6. Evidence of internal structure is covered in detail in Chapter 6, along with coverage of the statistical technique factor analysis. Briefly, internal structure evidence is considered to be supportive of a test's validity to the degree that the internal structure of a test mirrors that expected for the construct to be measured. When prior research or theory has suggested a certain structure for the construct of intelligence, extraversion, anxiety, speech articulation skills, and so on, a valid test is expected to show the same structure statistically.

As we noted in Chapter 4, evidence of a test's psychometric features is always based on a particular sample. When administering a test to examinees who differ markedly from that sample (which is typically the norm group), validity evidence from a test manual may not apply. This should prompt a search for research studies on the type of examinees you are testing.

Two Factors Affecting Validity Coefficients

Practitioners should be aware of two factors that can artificially reduce the size of validity coefficients, systematically underestimating the validity of tests. First, imperfect reliability in either the test or criterion will reduce validity coefficients. All measures, of course, have imperfect reliability, but for measures with genuinely low reliability (say, coefficients below 0.70), it's virtually impossible to obtain decent validity coefficients. This is another reason why reliability is important; it limits validity. Note that in criterion-related validity studies, both the test *and the criterion* must be reliable, a fact that is often overlooked when we choose criterion measures.

The second factor is restriction of range. All correlation coefficients are reduced by range restrictions, but this problem is especially significant when we are examining the predictive validity of selection measures. Consider a graduate program in psychology that uses the GRE quantitative section score as part of the data for making admissions decisions. The program generally requires a minimum score of 151, which is at about the 40th percentile of all GRE examinees. A university administrator challenges the use of the standardized admission test, and so the program decides to examine the predictive validity of the GRE among its students by correlating GRE scores with graduate school GPA (grade-point average). The scatterplot in Figure 5.2 shows the correlation data for the scores on the quantitative section of the GRE predicting graduate GPA in the most recent admitted cohort of 20 graduate students.

The correlation coefficient for the data in Figure 5.2 is $r = .24$, which is quite modest, but the statistic is misleading. Because the GRE scores are being used for selection, the GRE scores' range is restricted—the mean GRE score for the 20 admitted students is 158.75, which is at approximately the 68th percentile for all GRE takers. The applicants who were not admitted generally did not have as high GRE scores, and had they been admitted,

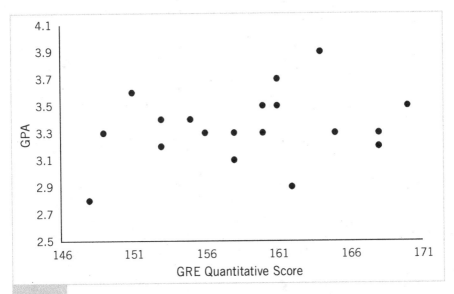

FIGURE 5.2. Scatterplot showing the relationship between GRE quantitative score and graduate GPA for 20 students admitted to graduate school.

they likely would not have done as well in graduate school. (Note that the range of the GPAs is also quite restricted; almost everyone has a GPA over 3.0.) If we added another 20 applicants who were rejected due to low GREs, and we looked at how they likely *would have performed* given the same correlation coefficient of $r = .24$, we would find something like the scatterplot of 40 total students shown in Figure 5.3.

The correlation coefficient for each subgroup of 20 students in Figure 5.3 (the 20 students who were admitted and the 20 who were rejected) is $r = .24$, but the coefficient for the full group of 40 students is $r = .60$, which indicates quite a strong predictive ability of the GRE! Of course, if the graduate program is using the GRE for selection (a reasonable decision, given the strong correlation), we would ironically never get to see the full dataset showing just how helpful the GRE is. As you can see, restriction of range can greatly mask the genuine validity level of tests.

Formulas are available to help take imperfect reliability and restriction of range into account when calculating validity coefficients, and in test manuals you will sometimes see a "corrected" r listed in validity tables. However, many test manuals do not consider these problems or only adjust for one of them. If you are concerned, particularly about restriction of range,

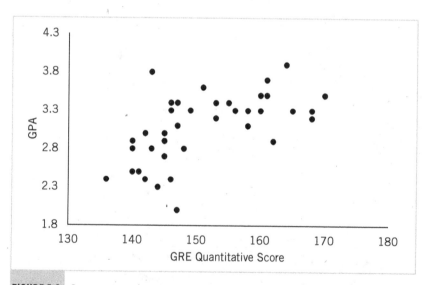

FIGURE 5.3. Scatterplot showing the relationship between GRE quantitative score and graduate GPA for 40 graduate school applicants (in those applicants who are not admitted, the expected GPA is estimated).

look at the standard deviation of the test scores in the validity study sample. If it is lower than the standard deviation of the normative sample for the test, you should mentally adjust the reported validity coefficient upward in a proportionate amount to get a better sense of the true validity.

Conclusions

Ultimately, validity is the most important quality in assessment. It means that the claims we make about examinees based on their test scores are accurate and justified. Validity evidence is never perfect even when it is strong, and the validation process continues long after a test is published. Every time a measure is used in a research study, we learn more about what that measure relates to, and this is our primary way of learning what construct(s) the measure is indexing. We should be rigorous when evaluating validity evidence, while also keeping in mind that decisions must be made about students and clients regardless of whether we use standardized assessment tools. Therefore, although we should choose the strongest tools available, making decisions with a tool with only moderate validity evidence is still far better than relying on our intuition.

APPLIED EXERCISES

1. A special education teacher is seeking a diagnostic mathematics test to use as part of a battery to identify learning disabilities in math in middle school students. She purchases the Test of Math Skills (TOMS). When reviewing the actual TOMS test materials (items), what might construct underrepresentation and construct-irrelevant variance look like? More generally, what sort of content validity evidence should the teacher seek? Finally, for convergent validity evidence, what relationships might be helpful to see in the TOMS manual?

2. A psychologist is using the CAARS, the adult ADHD symptom rating scale mentioned earlier in this chapter. The CAARS actually comes in two forms: one for the client to complete, and one for an "observer" (someone who knows the client well) to complete. The CAARS chapter on validity notes the correlations between self-report and observer-report scores on the scale. For instance, in a sample of female clients, test developers found that the self and observer data for one particular composite score, the ADHD Index, correlated at $r = .49$ (Conners et al., 1999, p. 72). How should this finding be interpreted? What kind of

TABLE 5.4.	Diagnostic Accuracy of a Hypothetical Screener for APD	
	Prior independent diagnosis of APD	No prior diagnosis
Test suggests APD	48	21
Test does not suggest APD	2	29

validity does it relate to? Is 0.49 a "good" correlation coefficient (i.e., one that shows good validity for the test)?

3. A speech-language pathologist is examining a new screening test for auditory processing disorder (APD), a condition that is typically diagnosed by audiologists but that speech-language pathologists routinely screen for. Among the test's validity evidence is data from a study in which 100 students with or without prior, independent diagnoses of APD were given the test. The data from the study are shown in Table 5.4; each number represents the number of study participants in that particular cell of the table. What are the sensitivity and specificity statistics for this test? How would you describe this classification validity evidence? Does it support this particular use of the test? Why or why not?

4. Choose an educational or psychological construct that you are familiar with: an area of cognitive ability, or an academic skill, a personality trait, or some type of psychopathology or other disorder or disability. Given what you know now about the types of validity evidence, as well as your background knowledge regarding the construct, what would be the optimal validity evidence for a test of the construct you chose?

CHAPTER 6

Factor Analysis

In Chapter 5, we saw that factor analysis relates to validity. Specifically, factor analysis provides evidence of the internal structure of a test—that is, which items, or subtests, or parts of a test relate to each other in stronger and weaker ways. Since most tests are designed to be multidimensional—that is, they are designed to measure multiple distinct constructs or traits—understanding how the parts of a test relate to each other is a type of validity evidence. Even when a test is designed to be unidimensional and only a single total score is generated, factor analysis can help to show that the test really is measuring a single unified construct. Although factor analysis is a sophisticated mathematical technique, and practitioners do not typically perform factor analysis calculations themselves, the technique is nonetheless important for practitioners to understand. Factor analysis data are found in most diagnostic test manuals, and those data can be very helpful in demonstrating the validity evidence for the test (and for the inferences we make on the basis of test scores).

Given the prominence of factor analysis in psychometrics, my goal is to discuss how to read and understand the factor analysis information that test users will see in test manuals without getting caught up in any unnecessary mathematics. The purpose of this chapter is not to show readers how to *do* a factor analysis (see Appendix A for resources on that), but to show how to *interpret* factor analysis data when deciding whether to use a test and which scores from the test are likely to lead to valid inferences.

This chapter focuses mainly on **exploratory factor analysis**, or **EFA**. In fact, when I refer to "factor analysis" without specifying any further, I'm usually referring to EFA. Test developers and researchers use EFA when they want to explore the internal structure of a test or battery of tests, without hypothesizing a particular expected structure ahead of time. The relationships between different parts of the test are investigated, but the goal isn't to just check whether one particular structure is present—the researchers are open to any possible structure. Later in the chapter, I will also discuss **confirmatory factor analysis**, or **CFA**. That technique is used to check how well the data on a test or battery fit a hypothesized internal structure. The researchers are, in essence, checking to see if the relationships between different parts of the test show what the hypothesized structure had predicted. A final note on terminology: EFA is quite similar to a procedure known as *principal components analysis* (PCA), and when reading test manuals, you might find that the evidence of internal structure actually comes from a PCA and not a factor analysis. For our purposes, I will treat PCA as a type of EFA, and you can apply the EFA discussion below to PCA data as well.

EFA: A Few Motivating Examples

One goal of factor analysis is to figure out what underlying constructs (or "factors") are causing variability in examinees' responses to test items. Even though the test items that clinical practitioners use are typically cognitive or psychological in nature, it is easiest to open with an example using a test of *physical* skills.

Example 1: The Decathlon

Consider the decathlon, the set of 10 track and field events that is over a century old. The 10 events are as follows:

1. The 100-meter run
2. The long jump
3. The shot put (pushing/throwing a very heavy ball)
4. The high jump
5. The 400-meter run
6. The hurdle race
7. The discus throw

8. The pole vault
9. The javelin throw
10. The 1,500-meter run

We could rate each athlete on each task on a scale from 1 (very poor performance) to 10 (excellent performance). This way, all ratings would measure skills in the same direction. If we did this for the performances of a large number of athletes who completed the full decathlon and then correlated the performance ratings between the tasks, where do you think the highest correlations would be? Where would the lowest correlations be? Take a moment to look at the list of 10 events and think about this before going on—which pairs of decathlon events are likely strongly (and positively) correlated? Which pairs are weakly correlated?

Most people, when asked this question, suggest that (for instance) the performance ratings from the 100- and 400-meter runs would be strongly correlated, whereas the ratings for the 100-meter run and the shot put would only be weakly correlated. Once you have thought some about these correlations, take the hypothetical study a step further: *why* are the tasks correlated to different degrees? More precisely, what are the underlying traits/constructs—the *factors* determining someone's performance on the various tasks? Again, take a moment to think about this issue: what physical traits/skills/abilities account for variation on the tasks?

People will often suggest such traits as upper body strength, leg strength, and speed. The tasks seem to cluster together naturally so that some tasks, like the shot put, rely heavily on upper body strength but not so much on the other factors. (Speed is not much of a factor in shot put performance.) The clusters would be the sets of tasks that are highly intercorrelated (within each set).

Of course, if we actually performed this study, we could use the data to better understand the factors underlying performance on each task. For instance, does performance on the hurdle race rely more on leg strength or speed? It seems to require both, but we could see if it correlates more with the other jumping tasks or with the other racing tasks. In addition, if we found that all the 10 tasks showed very high intercorrelations with each other, such data might suggest that a single factor—just one underlying trait—accounts for performance on the 10 tasks. If all of the intercorrelations were very low (close to zero), this might suggest that performance on each task depends on a different, distinct physical skill. In short, by examining the correlations, we would get a good sense of the structure of physical abilities measured by the decathlon. As we will see, factor analysis data will show which factor(s) a task "loads" on, and that is based on the set of correlations between all of the tasks.

Example 2: High School Grades

To return to the measurement of *mental* traits, consider the pattern of performance of a group of high school students in 11th grade. Another hypothetical study: we go to a large high school where all 11th graders take the following six classes:

1. English
2. History
3. French
4. Algebra
5. Geometry
6. Physics

We examine the numerical GPA of each student in each of the six classes at the end of the school year, and we correlate the GPA variables. This time, I will show some hypothetical correlation coefficients; see Table 6.1. Where do you see the clusters of higher and lower correlation coefficients? Again, take a moment to think about this.

TABLE 6.1. Correlation Coefficients for Relationships between Students' Grades in Different Subject Areas

	English	History	French	Algebra	Geometry	Physics
English	—					
History	0.70	—				
French	0.73	0.65	—			
Algebra	0.21	0.19	0.17	—		
Geometry	0.15	0.22	0.10	0.80	—	
Physics	0.13	0.07	0.20	0.85	0.75	—

You likely noticed that there are two sets of high intercorrelations. One set is among the first three classes: English, history, and French. The other set is among the second three classes: algebra, geometry, and physics. Grades in the first set of classes do not correlate much with grades in the second set of classes, but within each set, the correlations are high. It might be, then, that there are two general traits, or two factors, that affect grades in these 11th graders. To think about what those factors might be, we consider what the variables within each set have in common. What would be a good name for each set—a name that would *not* describe the other set well?

We could call the first set something like "humanities" and the second set something like "math/science." To take things a step further, we can ask about what traits account for the correlations. What skills are required a great deal in English, history, and French classes, but not algebra, geometry, and physics classes? For one thing, the English, French, and even the history class can involve a lot of reading of complex texts, so reading and language skills might be important. Meanwhile, math reasoning skills are obviously required in algebra and geometry, and they're required in physics as well. If this process sounds a bit subjective, that's a fair point. Naming factors is somewhat arbitrary, based on our best educated guess about what ties together the variables that show high intercorrelations with each other.

Factor analysis is used to analyze a correlation matrix like the one shown above and to identify patterns of higher and lower correlations. Why can't this be done by just "eyeballing" the matrix? Often, the patterns are not easy to see, especially in a large matrix or in a matrix where the list of variables does not have a clear order. Moreover, the patterns can be subtle and at times go against our expectations, so we don't always know where in the matrix to look. However, even the intercorrelation matrix itself is evidence of internal structure of the test, and often test manuals will present intercorrelations between subtests as validity evidence that supports the test.

Other Examples

The examples that I have given so far have come from athletic performance and school grades, but factor analysis is even more important (and more commonly used) in diagnostic testing. In that arena, the variables entered into the factor analysis are an examinee's scores on subtests or individual items. For instance, to perform a factor analysis on an academic achievement test consisting of two reading subtests, two math subtests, and two writing subtests, we could enter the six subtest scores. We would expect the two subtests within each area to correlate more highly with each other than with subtests in other areas. If we had a nine-item self-report scale measuring the nine official symptoms of a depressive episode (an instance of clinical depression), we could take the nine individual item scores and enter them into a factor analysis to see if (for instance) the physical symptoms of depression (e.g., changes in sleep patterns) are more strongly related to each other than to nonphysical symptoms (e.g., feelings of guilt and worthlessness).

Reviewing EFA Data

Even though test manuals commonly display matrices of the intercorrelations of subtests, the results of factor analyses look rather different. To understand why, it helps to have a general sense of the process of factor analysis. All factor analyses start with a set of variables and their intercorrelations. Those variables are typically the items or subtests from a test. Mathematically speaking, the goal of a factor analysis is to create a smaller number of new variables that can represent most or all of the variability seen in the original variable set. The new variables are the factors. We often interpret these factors as representing the underlying traits that determine performance on the original set of variables, but mathematically, the factors are just a more efficient, smaller set of variables.

You can think of each factor as a special kind of average of the set of the original variables. Take the example of school grades that I discussed above. If we have class marks of 11th graders in six high school courses, we could represent each student's school performance as a set of their six course scores, but it might be more efficient to simply give two broader averages of each student's "humanities skills" and "quantitative skills." The statistical technique of factor analysis can help to identify a smaller number of variables, and a particular factor analysis solution might yield two factors that look very much like humanities and quantitative skills. The two factors are each *weighted* averages of the full set of initial variables, where the weights are based on how strongly each class (e.g., English, history) correlates with the factor. Those weights are called the **factor loadings**. If English is the purest measure of "humanities skills," then grades from English class would have the highest weight. We would expect history and French grades to have fairly high weights as well, whereas the math and science course grades would not be given much weight in determining the "humanities skills" average. You can think of the factor loadings as representing the strength of the relationship between each initial variable (here, high school course) and each factor, somewhat like a correlation coefficient.[1]

When researchers and test developers perform an EFA, they make a number of choices about exactly how to run the analysis, and those choices have a large effect on what the results look like. However, a typical format for factor analysis results based on the high school grade data is shown in Table 6.2. The results show the factors, the factor loadings (the weights), and how much of the variability in the overall set of variables (here, 11th grade course marks) is explained by each factor. The computer program used to run the factor analysis can't actually name the factors. Instead, researchers look for what the variables with high loadings on each factor have in common, and they use their best judgment to name the factor. Looking at the factor loadings is easier than searching for clusters of high correlations in a correlation matrix. It looks as though "Factor 1" is what we have been calling the quantitative skills factor, and "Factor 2" is the humanities skills factor. In a published report of a research study, the table of results might have the factors named this way.

TABLE 6.2. Factor Analysis Results for the High School Grades Example

Variable	Factor 1	Factor 2
English	0.03	0.85
History	0.08	0.83
French	0.05	0.82
Algebra	0.89	0.04
Geometry	0.93	0.05
Physics	0.87	0.08
% of variance explained	53%	40%

[1] Depending on exactly how the EFA is conducted, sometimes the factor loadings will be equivalent to correlation coefficients.

If we wanted to apply the factor analysis results to an individual student, we could estimate their overall quantitative skills through a weighted average. For instance, we could take Sally's final numerical grade in each of her six classes, multiply each grade by the factor loading (the weight) in the Factor 1 (quantitative skills) column, and add those up. Technically, that sum would be called a **factor score**. If we did this for each student in the 11th grade, we would have an easy way to compare the students in their overall quantitative skills. However, three of the factor loadings—those for English, history, and French—are so low that they barely contribute to the weighted average. Indeed, the factor loadings show that those classes barely relate to the quantitative skills factor. Therefore, in practice, rather than calculating a factor score, we could instead calculate a quantitative skills index by just averaging the students' final grades in the three courses—algebra, physics, and geometry—that have the high loadings on the factor. That is, we would just use the factor analysis to identify which courses should be part of the quantitative skills index, but then calculate the index as the simple average of the final grades in that subset of courses. We can ignore the courses that barely relate to each factor.

You might be wondering why factor analysis would be used in the first place. Wasn't it obvious which courses should make up the quantitative skills index? Not necessarily. Without running the factor analysis, it wasn't clear that physics would load on quantitative skills almost as much as the math courses would. And what if some students took earth science instead of physics—would earth science also require high levels of quantitative skills? We could make a guess based on checking the earth science curriculum, but running a factor analysis would be far better. Moreover, we might want to make a genuine weighted average using factor scores so that we can estimate quantitative skills more precisely.

One final comment: the bottom line in the EFA results table is "% variance explained." The first factor found in an EFA is the one that accounts for the most variability in all of the original variables. Based on those EFA results, quantitative skills appear to account for the greatest amount of variability in 11th graders' class marks at that high school. The second factor will account for somewhat less variance. In theory, further factors can continue to be "extracted," but each will account for less variance than the former one, and since the sum total of variance explained must be 100%, at some point there isn't much advantage to extracting more factors. In this hypothetical example, the first two factors account for the vast majority (93%) of variance in students' class marks.

Factor Analysis and Diagnostic Testing

To see how EFA can be helpful when developing (and evaluating) a diagnostic test, consider a hypothetical test measuring oral language skills. We'll call it the Test of Oral Language Skills (TOLS). The TOLS has four subtests:

1. *Matching Sentences.* In each item on this subtest, the examiner shows the examinee three pictures. When the examinee hears the examiner say a sentence, the examinee must point to the picture that matches the sentence.

2. *Understanding Directions.* In each item on this subtest, the examiner asks the examinee to follow increasingly complex instructions (e.g., "Touch your nose with your finger; then open the book in front of you to page 5.").

3. *Creating Sentences.* In each item on this subtest, the examiner shows the examinee a picture. The examinee needs to say a sentence describing what is happening in the picture.

4. *Word Vocabulary.* In each item on this subtest, the examiner says a word (the words become increasingly advanced), and the examinee must provide a clear and accurate definition of the word.

In the normative sample, the intercorrelations between the TOLS subtests were those shown in Table 6.3, and an EFA on those correlations yields a two-factor solution shown in Table 6.4.

Since only four variables are entered in the factor analysis, it's easy enough to start out by eyeing the correlations themselves. The highest correlation is between Creating Sentences and Word Vocabulary; $r = .85$. The correlation between Matching Sentences and Understanding Directions is not far behind; $r = .78$. The rest of the correlations are considerably smaller—between .34 and .52. All of the correlations are positive, and with a reasonable sample size, they would all be statistically significant. This is

TABLE 6.3. Intercorrelation Table for the TOLS Example

	Matching Sentences	Understanding Directions	Creating Sentences	Word Vocabulary
Matching Sentences	—			
Understanding Directions	.78	—		
Creating Sentences	.34	.37	—	
Word Vocabulary	.52	.48	.85	—

to be expected; different oral language skills will positively correlate with each other. The tasks overlap somewhat as well, involving similar skills. But clearly, some of the subtests are much more closely related than others are.

The EFA results offer more clues to what's happening. The first factor has two subtests with high loadings—Matching Sentences and Understanding Directions. What do these subtests have in common with each other more than they have in common with the other subtests? It helps to know a bit about oral language skills, but the task descriptions suggest that neither subtest requires the child to speak. Therefore, those two subtests are relatively pure measures of *receptive language* (roughly, listening skills), without tapping *expressive language* (speech) much. We might tentatively guess that Factor 1 represents variability in receptive language skills. The other loadings on the first factor seem consistent with this explanation. The Creating Sentences subtest doesn't involve listening, and it has the lowest factor

TABLE 6.4. EFA Results for the TOLS Example

Variable	Factor 1	Factor 2
Matching Sentences	.80	.18
Understanding Directions	.73	.20
Creating Sentences	.24	.83
Word Vocabulary	.45	.59
% of variance explained	63%	28%

loading. Word Vocabulary does involve some listening (to the examiner saying the word) and comprehension of spoken words, and it has a moderate factor loading.

Meanwhile, the second factor shows its highest loading for Creating Sentences, which is quite speech-heavy (needing to create a whole sentence from scratch, inspired only by a picture), and Word Vocabulary, which also involves considerable speech. The second factor's two lower loadings are for Matching Sentences and Understanding Directions, two subtests requiring no speech at all. Given these results, the TOLS developers might call Factor 1 "Receptive Language" and Factor 2 "Expressive Language." Moreover, the developers could make composite scores for each skill area based solely on the two subtests with the highest loadings on each factor. There would be an overall Receptive Language composite score based on the sum or average of students' performance on Matching Sentences and Understanding Directions, and an overall Expressive Language composite score based on the sum or average of performance on Creating Sentences and Word Vocabulary. We would only count each subtest toward the composite score that it has its highest loading on. Finally, there would likely be an overall Oral Language score based on performance on all four subtests. This would in fact be a typical approach to test development.

To take another example, but one where the variables entered into the factor analysis are individual items, consider the Enculturation Scale for Filipino Americans (del Prado & Church, 2010)—a measure that I introduced in an example in Chapter 4. In its full form, the scale has 73 items, such as "I like to listen to music by Filipino musicians." Each item is rated on a 6-point scale indicating the amount of agreement with the item (1 = strongly disagree, 6 = strongly agree). EFA data suggested that there were three factors underlying the intercorrelations between the scale's 73 items. The scale developers concluded that the first factor involves the degree of connection that Filipino Americans feel with their homeland, and 29 items (including the sample item that I gave) primarily loaded on this factor. A second factor involves interpersonal norms for behavior associated with Filipino values (another 29 items primarily loaded here), and a third factor involves socially conservative beliefs (the remaining 15 items primarily loaded here). The scale developers created a subscale score for each factor by averaging responses to the subset of items that primarily loaded on that factor. A respondent would receive an overall score for the scale (the average of their responses to all 73 items) and three subscale scores as well.

Factor Analysis and Validity

Factor analysis relates to what we have called construct validity—that is, the degree to which a test measures the construct(s) that it claims to measure. As with most other validation strategies, we can compare factor-analytic evidence against other types of evidence of the construct(s) to see if they converge. One way to do this is to compare EFA results to those from prior research on the constructs. For instance, decades of research have shown that ratings of most personality traits can be grouped into five overall areas or basic trait dimensions known as the Big Five personality traits: Extraversion, Neuroticism, Agreeableness, Conscientiousness, and Openness to Experience (John et al., 2008). Therefore, if we constructed a lengthy self-report questionnaire that aimed to be a comprehensive assessment of general personality traits, we might expect an EFA to identify five factors where the item loadings would make the factors look roughly like the Big Five trait areas. Moreover, we could inspect the factor loadings of individual items to see if they "made sense," given what we know of each trait. For instance, one aspect of neuroticism is a tendency to worry and feel anxiety. If one of the items on the personality questionnaire was "I experience uncontrollable worry about many things in my life," we would expect its highest factor loading to be on the factor labeled Neuroticism (or something similar). If the item had a high loading under Extraversion but not Neuroticism, this would be unusual, and if we noticed not just one but many anomalies like this, the validity of the test would be called into question.

To take another example, it has been known for over a century that all cognitive ability tests show positive correlations with each other in large, representative samples (Schneider, 2013). However, some cognitive tasks correlate with each other more strongly than they do with others. For instance, one area of cognitive ability reliably found in factor analyses of cognitive tasks is known as *crystallized intelligence*, which refers to learned knowledge of different types. In an EFA of a diverse set of mental tests, we would therefore expect tests of vocabulary (with items like "What does the word *imitate* mean?") and general information (with items like "What city is the capital of Poland?") to load on the same factor, since vocabulary and general information are both aspects of crystallized intelligence. If we were designing an IQ test that included many different types of cognitive tasks, and vocabulary and general information did not load on the same factor, it would be very odd and would require some explanation, given what is already known about the structure of cognitive abilities.

In our earlier example of the hypothetical TOLS, we saw that the factor analysis "made sense." The two factors, expressive and receptive language, showed loadings for the four subtests that made sense given the task requirements on those subtests, and the proposed names of the factors also made sense. Consider instead if the TOLS's manual showed the EFA results seen in Table 6.5. These results would likely be distressing for the test developers. The two subtests that only require receptive language skills don't really load on the same factor, nor do the two subtests requiring substantial expressive language skills. Indeed, looking back at the descriptions of the four subtests, it's hard to think of any reason for why these results would appear. Admittedly, it's theoretically possible that there is a good reason why Matching Sentences and Word Vocabulary had very strong loadings on the same factor that Understanding Directions and Creating Sentences did not, but the test developers would have to make a reasonable argument for this pattern of loadings, and the factor names (and resulting interpretations) would need to reflect that argument.

More generally, whether factor analysis results are supportive of a particular test depends a great deal on what claims the test makes. At times, these claims involve the different scores that the test generates. For instance, the WISC-V (Wechsler, 2014) generates an overall Full Scale IQ score, as well as separate "index" scores for five different areas of cognitive ability: (1) Verbal Comprehension, (2) Visual–Spatial, (3) Fluid Reasoning, (4) Working Memory, and (5) Processing Speed. Each of the index scores is based on performance from two subtests in that area, and the Full Scale IQ

TABLE 6.5. Alternative Hypothetical EFA Results for the TOLS

Variable	Factor 1	Factor 2
Matching Sentences	.75	.11
Understanding Directions	.30	.54
Creating Sentences	.18	.83
Word Vocabulary	.84	.09
% of variance explained	56%	39%

is based on a total of seven subtests (one or two subtests from each of the five areas). The test is claiming, at least implicitly, that a test user can make valid inferences about not only an examinee's overall intelligence level, but also their level of those five distinct areas of intelligence. Optimally, a factor analysis on the 10 subtests that yield the five index scores would show five factors that account for almost all of the variance in test scores, and each pair of subtests that makes up an index score should have their highest factor loadings on the same one of the five factors. If an EFA failed to show these results, this might undermine the interpretation of some or all of the index scores (depending on exactly what the EFA results looked like), but the Full Scale IQ could still be valid and interpretable. At other times, a factor analysis might lead to questioning all of the composite scores on a diagnostic test, but the individual subtest scores could still be useful.

Factor analysis data, and internal structure evidence more generally, are just one source of validity evidence. As we discussed in Chapter 5, there are many other sources of validity evidence. Even if a factor analysis shows some deficiencies, these could be overcome by other types of validity evidence that strongly support an instrument. As with all things in psychometrics, we expect that tests will be imperfect, but psychometric evidence can quantify the imperfections and allow us to temper our confidence in inferences and decisions as needed.

Confirmatory Factor Analysis

Measurement Models

Generally, test developers and researchers already have a sense of what kind of internal structure they expect a test or battery to have. Even if they choose to run an EFA, there's often a particular structure that they expect the EFA to show. Sometimes that structure comes from prior tests, prior independent research, or theories that have been proposed about whatever constructs the test/battery is designed to measure. In CFA, a particular structure is explicitly specified, and the data are "fit" to the structure. The proposed structure is typically called a **measurement model**, and so we say that the model is tested (checked) by the CFA. A CFA will tell us how well the data fit that particular model. Often, researchers will run multiple CFAs for different models to see which model the data fit best.

One advantage of CFA is that it can make the interpretation of a factor analysis less subjective. You may have found it surprising—even a bit frustrating—to be told to view the EFA results and see if they "make sense." It does take thoughtful judgment to look at EFA results and draw conclusions about whether they seem to support the structure of the test that the developers claim is present. Now you can see that evaluating EFA results as a test user has a confirmatory aspect; you're trying to determine whether the typical, expected interpretations of the test scores (usually those proposed in the Interpretation section of the test manual) are supported by the structure of the test that the EFA shows. But the confirmatory aspect of EFA is a bit subjective, involving looking at tables of factor loadings and hoping that a meaningful pattern emerges. In contrast, formal CFA procedures allow the test developers to offer quantitative evidence of the precise degree to which their proposed structure fits the data.

At times, test manuals will display the measurement model(s) proposed by the test developers graphically. (Independent research studies almost always show such graphical displays.) For instance, the measurement model for our hypothetical language skills test, the TOLS, might look like Figure 6.1. In this measurement model, you can see how the four subtests relate to two hypothesized underlying traits (expressive and receptive language skills) and how those two traits relate to an overall underlying trait of general language skills. After a CFA is performed, the displayed measurement model may also show the quantitative relationships (similar to correlations)

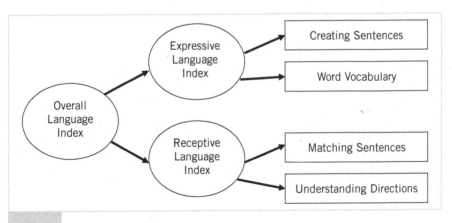

FIGURE 6.1. Measurement model for the TOLS.

between each of the variables and each of the other variables, so you may see numbers and more arrows on the figure.

If a CFA shows that the data fit the proposed TOLS measurement model well, this will help to justify use of distinct index scores for receptive and expressive language skills. A test user could interpret those scores with more confidence that the scores actually measure the skills they claim to measure. Similarly, the overall language index score could be interpreted as a truly general measure of both receptive and expressive language skills.

Fit Indices

The fit of CFA models is tested using fairly advanced statistics (even more advanced than most EFA procedures), but as a consumer of CFA results, there is no need to understand in detail the procedures behind their calculation, only how to interpret them. Computer programs used to run CFA procedures will generate many **fit indices**—that is, statistics designed to indicate how well the data fit the measurement model. I discuss some of the most common fit indices here.

The original fit index in CFA models was a chi-square statistic, usually symbolized as χ^2. This statistic is the result of an inferential statistical test performed to see whether the data and the measurement model are significantly different from each other. Therefore, if χ^2 is significant, it is not a particularly good thing for the model; the statistic has shown that the data are significantly discrepant from the hypothesized model. A nonsignificant χ^2 statistic is instead thought to be good news, news that the statistical test can't distinguish between the data and the model because the two are so close.

The χ^2 index is the only fit index that is a test of statistical significance, and like other inferential statistics, it is very sensitive to sample size. Indeed, with a very large sample size, even slight differences between the data and the measurement model will lead to a significant χ^2. This is unfortunate; test developers who do a good job of obtaining a large sample will be "punished" when their CFA tells them that their model is not supported by the data. Another downside of the χ^2 index is that it is interpreted in an all-or-nothing way; it's either significant or not significant, which doesn't allow for shades of gray.

Given the disadvantages just mentioned, the χ^2 index is rarely mentioned alone. A different index, the goodness-of-fit index (GFI), can be thought of as similar to a squared correlation coefficient, showing the overlap between the data and the model. Therefore, higher GFI values are better, with 1 being the highest possible, and values of at least .90 being desirable. Another index, the root mean square error of approximation (RMSEA) is a measure of the size of the discrepancy between the model and the data, and so lower scores are more desirable. Values of .08 or below are considered to indicate acceptable model fit. Table 6.6 lists these and many other CFA fit statistics and their typical interpretation. Different fit indices may not all point in the same direction (i.e., good or bad) for the model, and so researchers must make an overall judgment by looking at all of the available indices. Therefore, as a test user, when you view CFA information in a test manual, consider all of the indices that are reported, and ask yourself whether they show a good fit overall.

TABLE 6.6. Common Fit Statistics in CFA Research

Fit index	Abbreviation	Interpretation[a]
Chi-square	χ^2	Smaller is better; best to be nonsignificant, but highly dependent on sample size.
Chi-square over degrees of freedom	χ^2/df	Smaller is better; a value of 5 or less indicates acceptable fit; a value of 2 or less indicates good fit.
Root mean square residual	RMSR	Smaller is better; a value of .05 or less is desirable.
Standardized root mean square residual	SRMR	Smaller is better; a value of .05 or less indicates good/ excellent fit; a value of 0.08 or less indicates acceptable fit.
Root mean square error of approximation	RMSEA	Smaller is better; a value of .08 or less indicates acceptable fit; a value of .10 or above is generally unacceptable.
Goodness-of-fit index	GFI	Larger is better; 0.90 or above indicates an acceptable fit.
Adjusted goodness-of-fit index	AGFI	Larger is better; .90 or above indicates an acceptable fit.
Comparative fit index	CFI	Larger is better; .95 or above indicates a good fit; .80 or above indicates an acceptable fit.
Normed fit index	NFI	Larger is better; .95 or above indicates an acceptable fit.
Tucker–Lewis index	TLI	Larger is better; .95 or above indicates a good/excellent fit; .90 or above indicates an acceptable fit.
Akaike information criterion	AIC	Smaller is better.
Brown–Cudek criterion	BCC	Smaller is better.
Bayesian information criterion	BIC	Smaller is better.

[a]Interpretation comments gathered from Gunzler et al. (2021), Keith (2019), and Meyers et al. (2013).

As I noted earlier, often when CFA is used in test development and validation, multiple models are checked to see which model fits the data best. The fit indices mentioned above can be compared across models. If a test manual reports fit statistics for two models, and the fit for one model is acceptable whereas the fit for the other model is not, you should interpret scores according to the acceptable model. If both models have acceptable fit but one has better fit than the other, the model with better fit will lead to interpretations with more evidence behind them. Special statistical analyses can even be performed to determine if one model is (statistically) significantly better than another (i.e., a significantly better fit to the data). If those analyses are presented, test users can look for p-values under 0.05 (or even lower) indicating such significance.

A Real-World Example

The Clinical Evaluation of Language Fundamentals, Fifth Edition (CELF-5; Wiig et al., 2013), is a battery used to assess language functioning in children, adolescents, and young adults (ages 5–21). It includes many subtests and yields separate scores for them, as well as an overall Core Language Score based on some of the subtests. It also yields other composite scores based on different clusters of subtests. Two of the composites are the Receptive Language Index and Expressive Language Index scores. (The CELF-5 has notable similarities to our hypothetical test, the TOLS!)

The CELF-5 authors conducted a number of CFA analyses as part of the test's validation process. One CFA measurement model that was evaluated involved data from children ages 5–8. The model was hierarchical, with overall language skills (the Core Language Score) at the apex of the hierarchy, receptive and expressive language skills underneath that construct, and finally three subtests underlying each of the receptive and expressive areas. The fit statistics for this model are shown in Table 6.7. This is all of the CFA information that the manual provides for this particular model, and all of the interpretable fit statistics are at least acceptable, according to the criteria outlined above. If alternative models for the same subtest scores were presented, some of the additional indices (e.g., the AIC) could be compared across the models to see which indicated the best fit. Moreover, test users can check the individual subtests to determine whether the actual items require the skills that the measurement model claims each subtest measures.

TABLE 6.7. Fit Statistics from a CFA Performed on the CELF-5	
Fit index	Value
χ^2	26.23
χ^2/df	3.75
AGFI	.97
CFI	.99
TLI	.98
RMSEA	.06
AIC	54.23
BIC	119.81

EFA or CFA?

Increasingly, test manuals are restricting their internal structure evidence to (1) intercorrelation tables and (2) CFA results, without any actual EFA results. When this happens, the data presented in the manual may show an adequate fit for the theoretical structure and set of scores that the test developers suggest, but this would not necessarily be the *best* model for understanding the data. Often, after a measure is published, independent EFAs are conducted, and at times they suggest alternative interpretations of the test's scores.

For instance, as I mentioned earlier, the WISC-V offers index scores for five different areas of cognitive ability: Verbal Comprehension, Visual–Spatial, Fluid Reasoning, Working Memory, and Processing Speed. The WISC-V technical manual (Wechsler, 2014) presents CFA evidence that a five-factor model fits the intercorrelations well. However, independent EFAs have found alternate structures for WISC-V data. To take one example, Canivez and colleagues (2018) presented EFA results suggesting that fewer than five factors were needed to explain WISC-V subtest intercorrelations; alternate structures may account better for those intercorrelations. One implication for WISC-V users might be to focus on the overall (Full Scale) IQ score, which does not make the same structural assumptions as index scores. As Canivez et al. suggest, another implication might be for the test developers to provide alternative index scores based on a structure more consistent with EFA results. Although independently collected validation data are always helpful, the particular structure proposed by the test developers need not be the best structure; it just needs to fit well enough to support useful score interpretations. Again, internal structure evidence is just one type of validity evidence to review.

Conclusions

Although factor analysis data is based on advanced statistics, just a bit of background can help clinicians to properly interpret that data competently. Beyond providing evidence for (or against) the validity of various test scores, factor analysis data can also help to better understand the constructs themselves. When considering using a new test, it is worth taking some time first to inspect the intercorrelation tables in the manual and then to look at the correlation coefficients in relation to the subtest stimuli and tasks as a means of better understanding what they're measuring. Then, you should inspect any factor analysis information in the manual, perhaps with your own hypotheses of what you would expect to find, given the nature of the subtests, the composite scores offered by the test, and the intercorrelations you've already viewed. You will come away more informed about both the test and the traits that the test was designed to measure.

APPLIED EXERCISES

1. On the WISC-V, four of the subtests are the following:
   - *Similarities*—The child must say what pairs of concepts have in common (e.g., *ruler* and *stopwatch*).
   - *Vocabulary*—The child must give definitions for increasingly difficult words.
   - *Block Design*—The child must rearrange blocks to match pictures they are shown.
   - *Visual Puzzles*—The child must identify small pictures that, if arranged together, would make a larger picture.

   The first two of these subtests combine to yield the Verbal Comprehension Index score, and the second two subtests yield the Visual–Spatial Index Score. The intercorrelations between the four subtests (taken from the technical manual; Wechsler, 2014, p. 74) are shown in Table 6.8. How well do these

TABLE 6.8. Selected Subtest Intercorrelations from the WISC-V

	Similarities	Vocabulary	Block Design	Visual Puzzles
Similarities	—	.68	.46	.48
Vocabulary	.68	—	.47	.51
Block Design	.46	.47	—	.60
Visual Puzzles	.48	.51	.60	—

intercorrelations support having separate index scores for Verbal Comprehension and Visual–Spatial skills? Explain your answer.

2. The Abbreviated Math Anxiety Scale (AMAS) is designed to measure mathematics anxiety in college students in counseling and other settings. The instructions for the AMAS ask students to report how much anxiety they experience in nine different situations related to math. Hopko and colleagues (2003) developed the AMAS and performed a factor analysis on its nine items, yielding the two-factor solution seen in Table 6.9. (Each item describes a math-related situation in which someone might experience anxiety.) Based on these factor loadings, what might Factors 1 and 2 each represent? Explain your answer.

TABLE 6.9. EFA Data for the AMAS

Item	Factor 1	Factor 2
1. Having to use the tables in the back of a math book.	.52	.35
2. Thinking about an upcoming math test one day before.	.27	.86
3. Watching a teacher work an algebraic equation on the blackboard.	.77	.35
4. Taking an examination in a math course.	.22	.89
5. Being given a homework assignment of many difficult problems that is due the next class meeting.	.31	.66
6. Listening to a lecture in math class.	.86	.25
7. Listening to another student explain a math formula.	.82	.17
8. Being given a "pop" quiz in math class.	.29	.84
9. Starting a new chapter in a math book.	.75	.26

Note. From Hopko et al. (2003). Reprinted with permission from SAGE Publications.

3. The Test of Word Reading Efficiency, Second Edition (TOWRE-2; Torgesen et al., 2012), has two subtests, one involving reading a list of unrelated words aloud as quickly as possible (Sight Word Reading Efficiency) and one involving reading a list of *fake* words (e.g., *zeb*) as quickly as possible (Phonemic Decoding Efficiency). Each subtest comes in four versions, which allows TOWRE-2 users to repeatedly measure a student's skills. As part of the validity evidence for the TOWRE-2, the test manual presents results from a CFA measurement model with two factors (Sight Word Reading Efficiency and Phonemic Decoding Efficiency) and the four forms of each subtest under each of the factors. This model yielded the following fit statistics: $\chi^2 = 160.38$, Comparative Fit Index (CFI) = .99, Tucker–Lewis Index (TLI) = .99, RMSEA = .067. In addition, the manual notes that another model was tested with only a single factor and its fit was significantly ($p < .001$) poorer. Evaluate the CFA evidence supporting the interpretation of the two subtests as measures of distinct skills. Refer to the table on fit indices earlier in the chapter, as needed.

4. Consider a multidimensional construct from your professional field that has not been used as an example in this chapter. Describe a set of subtests (tasks) meant to measure the construct and create a hypothetical matrix of intercorrelations as well as a table of factor loadings that support an expected factor structure.

CHAPTER 7

Bias and Fairness

Standardized diagnostic tests, now a little over a century old, were initially developed to reduce bias and improve fairness in decision making. For instance, the French psychologist Alfred Binet developed the first IQ test in 1905 because he was aware that teachers might be biased in their judgments of their pupils' intelligence. It's ironic, then, that today standardized tests are the assessment tools most often accused of bias. Critics of tests rarely suggest alternative ways of making decisions that are free of bias, but their concerns nonetheless merit serious attention. Like any assessment tool, tests can certainly be biased or be used in an unfair manner. One advantage of tests, relative to other assessment tools, is their quantitative nature, which makes them quite amenable to research studies to detect bias and unfairness. In this chapter, I describe bias and fairness in assessment and the ways in which test developers and researchers investigate them.[1]

The Problem of Group Differences

Test bias and fairness would likely not be of much concern among the general public were it not for group differences in test scores. For many

---

[1] I focus on these topics as they arise in the context of diagnostic testing; they are also prominent in work on tests used for admissions, school accountability, and the like. Those types of tests are beyond the scope of this chapter, but many of the same principles apply.

observers, the existence of group differences raises the possibility of test bias against any groups found to have lower performance on cognitive measures or higher rates of problems on rating scales. On many cognitive and academic tests, Black and Hispanic examinees have sometimes, *on average*, obtained lower scores than White and Asian examinees (e.g., Weiss et al., 2019). The portrait for gender differences has been more complicated; male examinees have tended, *on average*, to outperform their female counterparts on some measures of math and spatial skills, whereas the reverse pattern has been found on some measures of reading and verbal skills (Halpern & Wai, 2020).

Understandably, group differences raise concerns about bias, since tests are used for selection, identification, and placement, and so group differences in test scores can lead to disparities in those outcomes. Group differences are certainly consequential at the societal level, and biases of various sorts are one potential source of group differences. However, group differences in test scores are logically distinct from test bias; each can exist without the other. For instance, on average, girls consistently receive higher school grades than boys do (Voyer & Voyer, 2014), but scholars do not generally suggest that teachers' grading practices are biased against boys (even though that is certainly one possibility). Similarly, bias can be present even without group differences, if a test obscures group differences that are genuinely present. For instance, if a rating scale of ADHD symptoms showed that equal proportions of boys and girls had clinically significant levels of symptoms, this would be (at the very least) inconsistent with decades of research showing ADHD to be far more common in boys, and test bias might well account for the *lack* of difference seen in the data.

Because group differences are not, in and of themselves, evidence of bias, a different definition of bias—one that can be tested scientifically—is needed. Before moving on, however, a final comment: I have stressed the "on-average" nature of group differences to remind readers that even where such differences exist, they are only differences between the *average* scores of groups. Members of all groups exist at all levels of score distributions, and the distributions for different groups (e.g., the score distributions of SAT scores for Black and White high school students) show tremendous overlap. Therefore, we typically cannot make any inferences about someone's test scores based on their group status, and we should always strive to treat examinees as individuals when making decisions on the basis of test scores or any other information.

Test Bias and Psychometric Validity

Psychometricians generally view test bias as being present when the meaning of the test score would change according to the examinee's group. If a test score means one thing for men and another for women, it would be biased to interpret the score in the same way for examinees of both groups. This issue relates closely to validity; we can say that bias is present when the validity of inferences made on the basis of the test score would depend on the examinee's group status. For instance, consider a test of visual–spatial skills, where examinees are shown sets of five similar pictures and must choose the two pictures in each set that are identical. If the test's instructions are administered in English, and a student who is not fluent in English does not understand the instructions, their resulting score will not lead to valid inferences about their visual–spatial skills, whereas the score could lead to valid inferences in other students who are fluent in English. We could then say that the test exhibits bias against students who are not fluent in English.

To determine if bias is present, test developers and researchers typically study whether test scores function the same way in examinees from different groups. The studies use many of the same strategies that we reviewed in Chapters 5 (on validity) and 6 (on factor analysis), but they are employed in separate samples from different groups to see if the results agree.

Bias and Criterion-Related Validity

In Chapter 5, we saw how a common test validation strategy involves correlating its scores with those of other measures. The test being validated can be viewed as a predictor variable, and another measure would be the outcome variable in the correlation. **Predictive bias** can be assessed by examining whether the correlation/regression features are the same across groups. More specifically, a lack of bias would lead to regression lines that are similar across the groups.

Say that researchers are concerned that teacher ratings of ADHD symptoms may exhibit racial bias, such that teachers overpathologize the behavior of Black children relative to White children, and recall more instances of ADHD symptoms (inattention, hyperactivity, impulsiveness) when the child is Black. Particularly if a school finds that teacher ratings of Black students tend to show greater reports of severe behavioral issues, bias is a hypothesis that the school may wish to investigate. After all, a teacher's judgment and recollection of student behavior may be based on construct-irrelevant factors, such as the students' academic performance and the teacher's emotional reactions to each child.

A criterion-related validation strategy for teacher ratings might involve sending a third-party, independently trained researcher into classrooms to conduct systematic observations of the students who teachers had also been asked to rate. The observer can watch and record instances of ADHD symptoms, which can serve as the criterion to correlate teachers' ratings with. Let's say that the scatterplot of the relationship (with a regression line) looks like Figure 7.1. The scatterplot shows a reasonable correlation between the two variables, but to see whether the teacher ratings are biased, we would need to analyze the data separately for Black and White students.

Say that we did conduct this separate analysis, and we found the pattern of data shown in Figure 7.2. The White students' data are in the dotted ellipse, and the Black students' data are in the solid ellipse. If it helps, imagine both ellipses filled with tiny dots, each representing a different student. The graph shows that, on average, Black students receive higher teacher ratings of ADHD symptoms (i.e., the solid ellipse is shifted to the right relative to the dotted ellipse), but they also have more independently

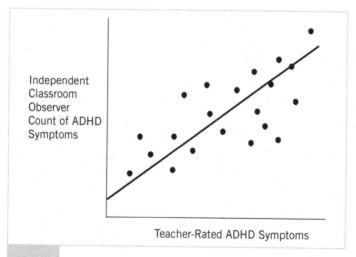

FIGURE 7.1. Scatterplot showing the relationship between teachers' ratings of students' ADHD symptoms and the symptom ratings made by independent observers visiting the students' classrooms.

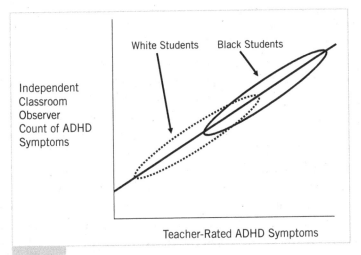

FIGURE 7.2. Schematic scatterplot showing group mean differences but no bias in teachers' ratings of students' ADHD symptoms.

observed ADHD symptoms (i.e., the solid ellipse is also higher on the graph than the dotted ellipse). The regression lines for Black and White students are the same; even though there are group differences in the rating scale data, the same group differences are seen in independently recorded observations. This graph would generally be interpreted as showing a lack of bias in teacher rating scales.

But maybe the data will instead look like those in Figure 7.3. There, the two groups of students have about the same level of independently observed symptoms (the two ellipses are about the same height on the y-axis), but the teacher rating scale scores are higher for Black students (the Black students' data are farther along the x-axis). These data might suggest that teachers are recalling and describing the Black students' behavior in more pathological ways, even though the Black and White students have the same independently observed behavior. This would generally be taken as evidence of bias in teacher ratings. Because the two regression lines reach the y-axis at different points, they have different y-intercepts, and the graph would be evidence of **intercept bias**. This bias clearly leads to a test score having different meanings for students from different groups. A teacher's ratings of a student would need to be "corrected" to account for the different regression lines, if the independent observers' records are taken as the gold standard of ADHD symptoms exhibited at school.

As yet another possibility, say that instead the data looked like those shown in Figure 7.4. There, the y-intercepts for the two regression lines are the same, but the lines are quite different in another way. They have vastly different slopes, and this graph would generally be interpreted as evidence of **slope bias**. The graph shows that among White students, higher teacher ratings correlate with higher numbers of independently observed classroom symptoms, but the same is not true among Black students. Instead, there is really no relationship between teacher ratings and observed symptoms among Black students; the teacher ratings don't appear to have validity for Black students and shouldn't be interpreted in the same way that they are for White students. Sometimes slope bias is less extreme but still present; a slope's steepness may be much lower for one group than for another, and so the test is less useful in the lower-steepness group.

Importantly, bias in criterion-related validity cannot generally be detected when the validity evidence is analyzed for all examinees together. The combined dataset might show reasonably good evidence of validity, but the measure might still be more valid for one group than for another (as in slope bias) or may predict a different level of a criterion for one group than for another (as in intercept bias). Therefore, analyses of test bias must be conducted separately from typical validity analyses.

More generally, criterion-related validity studies benefit from analyses that are conducted separately for participants from different demographic

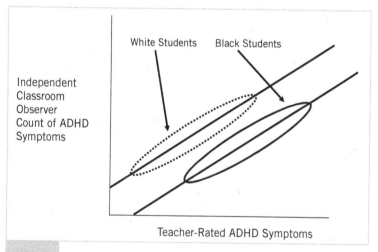

FIGURE 7.3. Schematic scatterplot showing intercept bias in teachers' ratings of students' ADHD symptoms.

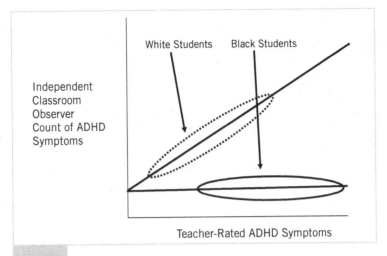

FIGURE 7.4.   Schematic scatterplot showing slope bias in teachers' ratings of students' ADHD symptoms.

groups. For instance, Tiburcio and Baker (2020) examined the validity of the third adolescent version of the Substance Abuse Subtle Screening Inventory (SASSI-A3). This inventory includes two types of items that suggest substance abuse—obvious face-valid items and "subtle" items asking about behaviors that are statistically associated with substance abuse and related traits. Tiburcio and Baker examined the SASSI-A3's criterion-related validity in 515 adolescents, using independent clinical diagnoses of substance abuse disorders as the criterion for comparison. The classification accuracy of the SASSI-A3 was calculated separately for adolescents from different ethnic groups: Black/African American (89% accurate), Hispanic American (91%), White/Caucasian (87%), multiracial (83%), and other (94%). These results show that the validity evidence of the SASSI-A3 was not limited to adolescents from a particular background, and the rates of classification accuracy were fairly consistent across ethnic groups, so this inventory did not show evidence of bias.

Internal Structure Evidence of Bias

In Chapter 6, we saw how factor analysis provides evidence of the internal structure of tests—evidence that helps to show validity. If a test is unbiased, it should generally have similar factor structures in different groups. One way to examine this is with exploratory factor analysis (EFA). Multiple EFAs are run, one for each group of interest (e.g., men, women), and the factors and factor loadings are inspected to check for discrepancies.

Say that a reading comprehension test finds substantial group differences in middle school students, such that girls outperform boys (e.g., $d = 0.50$). Researchers might want to check the factor structure of this test in girls and boys to ensure that it's measuring the same thing(s) in each group. Two EFAs are run, and both yield solutions where two factors explain most of the variance. There are 28 items on the test (those are the variables entered into the factor analysis), and half of the items were written to measure "literal comprehension" (the answers are found exactly in the reading comprehension passages), whereas the other half were written to measure "inferential comprehension" (the answers require students to infer things that are not directly mentioned in the passages). The factor loadings show that the items group nicely into the two categories; Factor 1 appears to measure literal comprehension, whereas Factor 2 appears to measure inferential comprehension. Almost all of the items written to measure literal comprehension have higher loadings on Factor 1 than on Factor 2, and for inferential comprehension, vice versa. More importantly, this pattern of loadings is found in the separate EFAs for boys and for girls. This evidence suggests that the constructs being measured are the same across groups, thereby mitigating concerns about bias.

Confirmatory factor analysis (CFA) is used in much recent research on test bias. Researchers can run multiple CFAs using the same model for multiple groups, checking to ensure that the model is a good fit for all groups. However, more sophisticated CFA techniques can actually be used to determine whether the factor structure is significantly different. These techniques are employed in **measurement invariance** studies, where **factorial invariance** is specifically sought. The studies check to see if a test or scale's functioning varies across groups, and they can be used to see if the factor structure in particular is invariant.

Whisman and colleagues (2013) conducted a measurement invariance study on the Beck Depression Inventory, Second Edition (BDI-II), a popular self-report measure of clinical depression symptoms with 21 items. These investigators first ran a variety of CFA models for the data from thousands of college students as a single sample. They found that the data were consistent with three clusters of items (three factors): the areas of "negative attitude" (e.g., pessimism about the future), "performance difficulty" (e.g., inability to make decisions), and "somatic elements" (physical symptoms such as fatigue). More specifically, the data were consistent with a hierarchical measurement model containing an umbrella factor of overall depression symptoms, the three factors just named under that, and then all of the 21 items clustered under the three factors. The researchers then used a special set of CFA procedures to test the equivalence of that model across gender and racial/ethnic groups. The logic of these special CFA procedures is complex, but essentially, they use CFA fit statistics to determine if the data are better accounted for by identical factor structures across groups than by different factor structures. The researchers observe if the fit statistics get substantially worse when the factor structures are forced ("constrained") to be identical. Whisman and colleagues found that the BDI-II exhibited measurement invariance across groups; the fit statistics did not decline appreciably with forced equivalent factor structures (the constrained models). These data suggest that the BDI-II measures the same traits across different gender and racial/ethnic groups, addressing concerns about possible test bias.

Differential Item Functioning

At times, although a test may not be biased as a whole, individual items may still exhibit bias. A variety of statistical methods can be used to detect **differential item functioning (DIF)**, which raises the *possibility* of bias. When DIF is present, the probability of two examinees from different groups responding the same way to an item will differ, *even when the two examinees have identical levels of the trait that the test is expected to measure*. For instance, math problems that use sports examples may be biased against female test-takers, who may be less familiar than male test-takers (on average) with sports. Say that a 30-item math subtest from an achievement test battery includes one item relating to comparing batting averages in baseball, and a test developer worries that the item could exhibit gender bias. The item would indeed exhibit DIF if two examinees (one male, one female) who are *equivalent in math skills* had a different chance of getting the item right. This could raise the possibility that the item is biased against female examinees. Again, DIF is not the same as bias per se; it only shows that some factor other than the trait that the test as a whole is measuring is affecting response patterns to a particular item, and demographic groups differ on that factor. Since that factor *might* be irrelevant to the construct that we wish to measure, the DIF could indicate construct-irrelevant variance for one group more than another group, which would be a case of psychometric bias.

DIF is investigated using a number of sophisticated statistical methods, mostly item response theory (IRT) models, discussed in Chapter 4. However, all DIF detection methods involve first estimating examinees' trait levels. Often, the estimate comes from the examinees' responses on other items from the test or from their total score on the test. Then, the percentage of examinees from each group at each trait level responding in a particular way to the item is calculated, and the overall pattern of item response behavior for each group is inspected to determine if it is substantially different across groups. Some of the DIF detection methods also allow for statistical significance testing to see if the item functioning is significantly different across groups. In our example above, if girls and boys who received the same total score on the test had different likelihoods of getting the sports-related item correct, this would be evidence of DIF.

Test manuals and research studies will often report DIF results in percentages—the proportion of items on the test that were found to exhibit either statistically significant DIF or DIF of a certain size. It is common and expected for a small proportion of items on a test to show DIF, just by chance. However, if a large number of items on the test show DIF, and particularly if the DIF is generally in the same direction (suggesting possible bias against one group), this would be a disadvantage of the test. All other things being equal, the test would not be preferred when assessing a diverse set of examinees.

DIF is often evaluated throughout the test development process, and items with significant DIF are eliminated before the test is published. For instance, on the Test of Integrated Language and Literacy Skills (TILLS; Nelson et al., 2016), DIF was examined during three field tests of items, and the test developers were able to remove almost all items showing DIF. In the final published version of the TILLS, across all 15 subtests (with hundreds of items in total), only four items showed DIF for gender, and none showed DIF for race or socioeconomic status.

Contrasting Bias with Other Problems

Bias versus Group Differences

As we noted earlier, bias is not the same thing as group differences in test performance. This point should be reinforced and expanded. Group differences can be caused by a variety of factors, and ruling out test bias does not endorse any other particular explanation of the differences. For instance, many measures of clinical depression find that women have higher rates of depression than men do. Biological factors and sociocultural factors both appear to play some role in these differences (Yoon & Kim, 2018). To assume that the measures of depression must be biased would be tantamount to ignoring factors that uniquely or differentially impact women's mood symptoms and that might suggest gender-specific treatment strategies. Acknowledging group differences can therefore be the first step in addressing disparities between groups.

Group differences in scores on cognitive and achievement tests also contribute to group disparities in rates of disability diagnosis, special education placement, personnel selection, and admission to educational institutions. Obviously, such disparities can be surprising and unwelcome, but their implications for test bias are not always clear. Consider a community college that uses a diagnostic test of math achievement to determine which students need remedial math before taking a required college algebra class. Black students are found to pass the placement test at lower rates than White students. The test has clear disparate consequences: Black students are more likely than White students to be forced to pay for a noncredit remedial math class before being allowed to proceed. But does this mean that the test should not be used? And if students are not required to take remedial math, will the long-term outcomes (e.g., failing college algebra and perhaps deciding not to continue in college) be even more disparate? These are complex questions; decision makers must consider analyses of how important remedial math really is, whether college algebra should itself be required, and whether noncredit remedial courses should even have a fee. Moreover, these questions are separate from whether the test is biased. Again, test users must always be sensitive to the consequences of testing, but those consequences do not make the test biased (or invalid) per se.

Bias versus Offensiveness

At times, accusations of bias are made against tests due to item content that some may find offensive, causing distress or discomfort. However, this is not the same as bias. Content that upsets some examinees may still lead to valid inferences, even about those examinees who experienced negative emotions in reaction to the content. Part of the difficulty here is that individual reactions to tests vary a great deal, and what is perceived as offensive changes over time, sometimes quite rapidly (Haslam, 2016). Regardless, systematic studies are always needed to document whether bias actually resulted from insensitive content.

In a fascinating recent study, Dee and Domingue (2021) analyzed the effects of an essay question that some viewed as racially insensitive, even "traumatic." The item appeared on an exam section administered on the second day of a two-day state language arts exam. Tenth graders in Massachusetts were asked to write an essay from the perspective of a White character in the novel *The Underground Railroad*. The researchers were able to compare Black and White students' performance on day 2 of the exam, while controlling for their first-day performance (prior to seeing the potentially offensive content). The researchers found only a tiny difference (.061 standard deviations) that was also common on prior exams without any reported offensive content. This finding suggests that even though the item may have been offensive to some, it had no systematic effect on test performance leading to biased estimates of skill levels.

This discussion is not meant to minimize the problem of offensive testing material. In fact, test developers can and do try to avoid offensive content. The most common strategy involves employing a **sensitivity review panel** composed of diverse stakeholders (Camilli, 2006). The panel reviews material both to try to ensure that offensive content is not on the test and to more generally encourage material that represents the perspectives, experiences, and contributions of a variety of groups of people. Optimally, members of the panel also have subject matter expertise related to the constructs that the exam is designed to measure. For instance, as the Gates–MacGinitie Reading Tests were being developed, 15 consultants from school districts and universities who were also members of five different ethnic groups reviewed reading passages and questions. Test material that was identified as potentially biased or offensive was generally either revised or reconsidered for inclusion on the test forms (MacGinitie et al., 2002).

Test publishers also aim to be responsive to concerns regarding item content after a test is released to the public. For instance, a major psycho-educational testing battery in use in 2001 had a drawing of a New York City skyline that included the Twin Towers and an airplane flying near them. After the September 11, 2001, terrorist attacks, out of concern that the image could cause distress, the publisher released an alternate drawing. More recently, concern about a drawing of a noose on a measure of language functioning caused the publisher to release a sticker of a drawing of a boomerang to place over the noose (Salo et al., 2022), given the noose's historical association with lynching of Black Americans. In both of these cases, there were no data showing any effects of the potentially upsetting stimuli on performance, but test developers took reasonable steps to avoid causing unnecessary distress to examinees, regardless of whether the test items are actually biased in the psychometric sense.

There is one important exception to the general strategy of offensiveness prevention: at times, sensitive topics are part of the target construct being measured. For instance, when assessing symptoms of clinical depression, asking about suicidal thoughts and intentions gets at a core symptom of depression and should not be left out of an assessment for fear of causing offense. On the other hand, if a reading comprehension test were being developed, it is unlikely that a reading passage including a graphic description of suicide would be chosen for inclusion, since coverage of suicide would be gratuitous and unrelated to the target construct.

Bias versus Social Disadvantage

Consider the following situation: an intelligence test is being given to a 6-year-old boy who has endured substantial social disadvantage throughout his life. He had inadequate medical care in his first few years, including recurrent ear infections that were not treated properly and likely affected his language development. He had little social stimulation prior to school starting, having been mostly taken care of by his grandmother who was herself medically compromised. He was almost never read to, and he had few experiences outside his home. High levels of street crime in the neighborhood where he grew up made it even more difficult for his single mother to want to spend much time with him outside. If he does poorly on the intelligence test, it would seem obvious that his upbringing has affected his performance. But does this mean that the intelligence test is biased? Probably not, although it would depend on the inferences being made on the basis of the test score. If a special education team infers that the boy's cognitive functioning is lower than that of most children his age and that he should receive additional assistance and educational services (typical inferences based on an intelligence test), those inferences would be no less valid for this particular examinee just because of the social disadvantage he has endured. Instead, we might say that social disadvantage has depressed his cognitive functioning, which the test has accurately measured.

At times, then, tests serve partially as indices of social disadvantage, including disadvantage caused by prejudice, large-scale societal inequalities, and the like. This does not make the tests biased, because social disadvantage is only affecting test scores *by affecting the constructs that the tests are designed to measure*. Tests are not designed to simply produce good news; often the purpose of diagnostic tests is instead to identify problems, and some of those problems are socially caused. But the tests are not themselves the causes of the problems. Indeed, as the National Council on Measurement in Education (NCME; 2019) has noted, "criticizing test results for reflecting . . . inequities is like blaming a thermometer for global warming."

A type of bias can creep into the situation when test users make *invalid* inferences on the basis of scores—inferences that make unwarranted assumptions about the causes of test scores. If the special education team in the example above inferred that the boy's IQ test performance showed his inherent cognitive limitations and concluded that he was unlikely to benefit from educational services, this would be an invalid inference, particularly because the social disadvantage seems to have had an effect here. When social disadvantage leads to lack of validity in inferences, bias is present in some sense, but even then, the bias is not really in the test per se. Instead, biased decision-makers are misinterpreting a test score.

Fairness in Test Use

Fairness is a much broader topic than bias; a test may be free of bias, as technically defined above (e.g., no evidence of predictive bias, no items with DIF), and yet it still may be used in a manner that is unfair to certain individual examinees. Regardless of the impressive technical qualities listed in the test's manual, it can still be misused, and this is a central concern of fairness. As test users, practitioners have a special responsibility with regard to fairness in diagnostic testing.

Opportunity to Access the Test

To perform well on a cognitive test, an examinee must possess two sets of skills. First are the **target skills**—the skills that the test is designed to measure. To do well on a (valid) test of math reasoning skills, the examinee must possess good math reasoning skills. To do well on a (valid) measure of receptive language, the examinee must have good skills in that area. Second are the **access skills**—the skills needed to participate fairly in the test, so as to facilitate a valid score. On a typical, paper-and-pencil test of math reasoning skills, the examinee must be able to read and understand the items. Even though the test is not designed to measure reading skills, such skills are simply assumed to be present, and an examinee lacking reading skills will not be able to fairly show their level of math reasoning skills. On a typical measure of receptive language that involves pointing at pictures in response to verbal instructions, the access skills include vision. Visually impaired examinees with excellent receptive language skills might do poorly on the test if they cannot see the test stimuli.

This analysis can be extended beyond cognitive tests to measures of personality and psychopathology. For instance, completing a self-report rating scale of anxiety symptoms and receiving a valid score requires access skills as well: vision/reading skills, and at least a minimal level of sustained attention capacity. An examinee's score on the scale can be affected both by the target construct (anxiety symptom levels) and by the levels of access skills. We typically assume that all examinees have the needed access skills, so that there will be no construct-irrelevant variance in test scores due to variability in these skills. However, this is not always the case. Two groups of examinees who are particularly prone to lack access skills are individuals with disabilities and individuals with limited proficiency in English. In addition, younger children and individuals from different cultural backgrounds may not always understand test instructions (another access skill).

Part of fairness in assessment is working to ensure that examinees have the opportunity to access tests so as to show whatever levels of target constructs they possess. One strategy for promoting fairness involves *selecting* appropriate tests. For instance, if a clinician is measuring math reasoning skills in a student known to be a poor reader, an orally administered test can be chosen. At times, a clinician might choose to only administer certain subtests from a battery, for similar reasons. Some diagnostic tests are available in multiple languages, although the clinician (or an interpreter) must also be fluent in the examinee's language. Unfortunately, many diagnostic tests do not include a convenient list of access skills in their manuals. Therefore, competent clinicians must be familiar with the task requirements of a variety of tests to understand which access skills are needed on each test and make thoughtful decisions about whether a particular test is appropriate for a particular examinee.

Another strategy for ensuring access involves adapting the administration of the test in some way, altering its task requirements. These changes to test administration are often known as **testing accommodations** (Lovett & Lewandowski, 2015).[2] For instance, *presentation accommodations* alter the test stimuli in some way, perhaps by reading items aloud to the examinee rather than having the examinee read the items to themselves. *Response format accommodations* alter what the examinee must do to respond to an item, such as allowing them to type rather than speak their answers to questions. *Setting accommodations* change the external environment in some way, such as altering the lighting conditions or using a special distraction-reduced testing space. Finally, *timing and scheduling accommodations* might give an examinee more time to respond to items or only schedule testing sessions early in the day.

Accommodations are a common approach to assisting students on classroom exams, as well as on high-stakes exams for school accountability, admissions, and certification or licensure. However, caution and care must be used when making alterations to test administration, particularly for diagnostic tests. Diagnostic tests are typically designed to assess disability conditions and the functional limitations that accompany them, so it is important that an accommodation not prevent a test from measuring a disability relevant to the target constructs on the test. More generally, accommodations are only appropriate if they address deficits in access skills *without altering the target skills needed for the test*. For instance, if a student with a severe learning disability in reading needs items from a math reasoning test read to her, this might be an acceptable accommodation, since the math reasoning test does not include reading skills among the target constructs. However, reading the items from a reading comprehension test to the same student would be inappropriate, since the test would then no longer measure reading comprehension (it would now measure listening comprehension).

Accommodations on diagnostic tests of cognitive, academic, speech/language, and neuropsychological functioning are generally reserved for examinees with sensory or physical disabilities, since sensory and physical

---

[2] Some measurement professionals distinguish between accommodations and *modifications*, with accommodations keeping the target construct intact and modifications compromising its measurement in some way. I find this distinction unhelpful, since whether something is an accommodation or a modification can depend on the particular test and examinee. I refer to all of these alterations as accommodations. See Lovett and Lewandowski (2015, chap. 1) for more discussion on this point.

skills are rarely part of the target constructs measured by mental tests. On measures of personality and psychopathology, accommodations are less often needed, but administration instructions typically have more flexibility built into them. Regardless, if any exceptions to standard administration conditions are made, they should be clearly documented on the test protocol and included in any resulting evaluation report.

A final strategy for addressing access issues, when test selection and accommodation processes are inadequate or inappropriate, is to alter the inferences made on the basis of test scores. At times, this can be as simple as acknowledging, when sharing or reporting scores, that the examinee's disability, language proficiency, or other status may have impacted certain scores, and that poor performance or unusual test responses could be related to either the target constructs or access skills. Test users might also caution about making decisions on the basis of scores. For instance, when considering an ADHD diagnosis, clinicians should not rely on self-report rating scales of ADHD symptoms in an adult who was later found to have a reading problem and might not have understood the items on the scales. In extreme cases, where test scores are inexplicably low or responses to items are bizarre, test users may need to caution against interpreting the tests at all. They can note in a report that the test was given, but that the results did not appear to be valid, with some explanation for why this might be the case.

Showing Respect for Examinees

Fair assessment practices show respect for examinees as individuals and grant examinees as much agency (freedom of choice) as possible in the testing process. Clinicians do this in several ways. First, as a general rule, clinicians ensure that clients have some understanding of why an assessment is taking place. There are exceptions for very young children or individuals with severe cognitive disabilities, but generally clinicians can convey the purpose of an assessment in a developmentally appropriate way. Second, except in very rare situations (e.g., emergencies), clinicians obtain consent for an assessment from either the examinee or a parent or legal guardian. The individual giving consent should understand in general what the assessment process will be like (e.g., what domains of functioning will be assessed). Third, where possible, clinicians emphasize the examinee's agency over issues such as whether to take a rest break or even in what order some assessment activities will take place. Finally, clinicians work to build rapport with examinees. Clinical assessment is generally a one-on-one process, where the clinician should convey sincere interest in forming a helping relationship with the examinee. Although attaining rapport can sometimes be challenging, either due to the context of assessment or the traits of the examinee, empathy and humility can go a long way toward showing examinees that the clinician is also a human being with the potential to provide useful assistance. A positive professional relationship between the clinician and the examinee can also lead to more valid scores, an issue that I discuss in more detail in the next section.

Ensuring Response Validity

Tests are not being used fairly with examinees if the tests systematically underestimate the examinees' skills or distort their true levels of constructs in other ways. If examinees do not put forth sufficient effort on cognitive tests, and if they or their informants are not entirely honest on questionnaires and rating scales, distortion will be the result. It is therefore of the utmost importance to motivate examinees to put forth adequate effort and to promote honest reporting of symptoms. Clinicians should also try to confirm whether effort and honesty were sufficient for valid inferences to be made on the basis of scores. **Response validity** is an umbrella term that encompasses both **performance validity** (adequate effort on cognitive tasks) and **symptom validity** (honest reporting of symptoms). **Response bias** refers to some type of failure of response validity. In forensic psychology and neuropsychology, these issues have been discussed widely for some time, and they are coming to be more widely understood as central to valid assessment in all areas of functioning (cf. Lovett et al., 2022).

The strategies discussed in the prior section on respect for examinees can help to increase response validity. As for detecting response bias, occasionally extreme versions are obvious: a child refuses to complete an assessment or gives silly responses with open sarcasm. Clients who show clear signs of fatigue or sleepiness during an evaluation should also raise concerns. Occasionally, an examinee's behavior should raise suspicions of response bias for other reasons. I recall one adult client who, when asked what his areas of concern were, "spontaneously" reported the nine inattentive DSM symptoms of ADHD in the order that they appear in the manual. More often, when response validity is compromised, data from testing will be discrepant from other sources of evidence (e.g., clinical observations, records of real-world performance in the examinee's clinical or school file).

There are also specialized assessment procedures (tests or parts of tests) that can detect response bias. *Performance validity tests* are very easy cognitive tasks; they can be performed well even by people with significant neurological challenges, but they are quite sensitive to any lack of effort or willful exaggeration of impairment. For instance, on the Test of Memory Malingering (TOMM; Tombaugh, 1996), the examinee views a series of simple line drawings. Then, the examinee is shown pairs of drawings; each pair contains one drawing already viewed and one new drawing, and the examinee is asked which drawing they had already seen. Even random guessing will lead to a 50% correct score, and so scores lower than this suggest that the examinee may be deliberately giving wrong answers. *Symptom validity tests* are lists of items, typically embedded in genuine clinical measures of psychopathology, whose endorsement suggests either careless responding or attempts to under-play or exaggerate true symptom levels. For instance, if an examinee circles "true" for an item that says "My commute to work takes 5 hours in each direction," it is unlikely that the examinee is filling out the questionnaire carefully. Similarly, if an examinee endorses several very severe symptoms, each of which is rare and associated with a different psychiatric disorder, the endorsement may suggest a desire to exaggerate one's problems.

It may seem odd to cover response bias as part of test fairness, but it does examinees no favor to credulously report scores that are invalid, even if the examinees may have wanted to produce such scores. Moreover, response bias occurs due to a complex set of reasons, including genuine psychopathology and fatigue/medical illness, as well as deliberate attempts to exaggerate impairment. To make inferences and decisions in our clients' best interests requires the most accurate knowledge about their construct levels, and so response validity is a key to treating each examinee fairly as an individual. Detecting response bias is sometimes the first step in determining a client's true problems.

Conclusions

Bias and fairness have been a concern in mental testing since its start over a century ago, and these issues remain a focus of criticism of testing by the public. Thankfully, test developers and researchers have developed a wide variety of techniques for detecting bias. Some of these techniques are employed even before a test is published in order to eliminate items that may be biased against various groups. Relatedly, procedures are typically used to identify and remove insensitive material. Group differences in test scores often remain and have a wide variety of causes, including social disadvantage. A key to understanding test scores is that the scores do not pass moral judgment on an examinee. Thus, even when an examinee scores poorly on a diagnostic test, revealing some kind of problem, this is not an examinee's "fault." At times, it *is* the fault of the testing process, and skilled clinicians can do a great deal to prevent this error. Selecting appropriate measures, making appropriate accommodations when needed, and acknowledging potential response validity issues when drawing inferences about examinees are all hallmarks of good practice.

APPLIED EXERCISES

1. You are reviewing test scores from an intelligence test that you have never heard of, the Morton Test of Intelligence (MTOI). The test has six subtests, three of which are designed to measure verbal/language/crystallized areas of cognitive ability and three of which are designed to measure nonverbal/visual-spatial/fluid areas of ability. The test scores you're looking at were obtained by an African American client, and you want to ensure that the MTOI does not exhibit bias against African Americans. As you locate research on the MTOI, what kind of evidence would optimally reassure you? Be specific about what studies might have been done with the MTOI looking at predictive bias, internal structure evidence of bias, and DIF, and what results of the studies would look like if the data were supportive of the test (and generally suggested a lack of bias).

2. You are a counselor reviewing results from a diagnostic assessment with a 16-year-old girl (the examinee) and her mother. The girl scored very high on the borderline personality traits subscale from a self-report clinical inventory. As you give this feedback and explain what borderline personality traits are, the mother becomes upset and says, "That sounds like any 16-year-old girl! Your test is biased against girls, I bet!" You know that the test norms do show a gender difference, with adolescent girls scoring higher than adolescent boys on the borderline traits subscale. How do you acknowledge this group difference to the mother while explaining that it's not the same thing as test bias?

3. A middle school student with a learning disability in mathematics is being reevaluated to get updated diagnostic data, and the evaluation includes three

math-related subtests from the Woodcock–Johnson IV Tests of Achievement (Schrank et al., 2014): *Calculation* (numerical problems starting with arithmetic and going into algebra and beyond), *Applied Problems* (responding to word problems of increasing complexity), and *Math Facts Fluency* (responding to as many single-digit arithmetic problems as possible in a short amount of time). The student tells you that he gets to use a calculator on his tests in class, and indeed, the accommodation is listed on his special education plan. He asks to use the calculator on the math subtests from the Woodcock–Johnson. How would you make this decision and explain it? Does it depend on the subtest? Think this through in terms of target skills and access skills. In addition, if an accommodation were made, how would this change what inferences could be drawn from the resulting test scores?

4. You are administering a cognitive test to a child in elementary school. The student seems tired, and she often says "I don't know" in response to test questions, without seeming to try to think of an answer. You ask if she's feeling okay and she responds that everything is fine, but the testing behaviors continue. You are concerned about performance validity. How might you detect response bias here, and how might you encourage greater effort? Is there anything else you can do?

CHAPTER 8

Sharing Test Results

As test users, our responsibilities do not end after scoring and interpreting someone's test performance. In some ways, our most challenging task is to convey the meaning and implications of test results to other parties: the examinee, family members, teachers, administrators, and a variety of other professionals who might work with the examinee. Feedback often starts with an oral conversation emphasizing the most important highlights of an evaluation; this oral presentation is followed by a written report that readers can review at their leisure and retain as a record to share with other professionals. The quality of this feedback determines whether our recommendations are likely to be implemented and whether clients, families, and fellow professionals view our conclusions as being well founded.

Entire books are available on report writing (see Appendix A for more resources). This chapter focuses specifically on how to share *test results* (as opposed to other information from a clinical evaluation). In addition, I spend more time than is typical discussing oral feedback; this somewhat neglected activity can help to frame audiences' understanding of the written report.

I follow four case studies throughout the first portion of this chapter to illustrate principles across several different types of assessment situations. (Often, after covering a principle, I only give examples from the more relevant cases.) The cases are as follows.

Case A: Ashante, a 12-year-old African American girl, is referred to the school psychologist in November of sixth grade for concerns related to inattention and possible ADHD. Her mother made the initial referral, but her teacher also acknowledges difficulties.

Case B: Blake, a White 7-year-old boy, is referred by his teacher to the special education team for concerns related to reading. He has almost finished first grade, but his teacher reports that he can only read about 30 simple words consistently and has extreme trouble sounding out words. A special education teacher (who also has a reading specialist credential) is in charge of assessing academic skills.

Case C: Carmen, a 4-year-old Mexican American girl, is being evaluated by a speech-language pathologist through an early intervention services program in her county, due to concerns about language development. She just turned 4, and she only speaks in one-word (and occasionally two-word) sentences.

Case D: Daiki, a 20-year-old Japanese American man, is finishing his sophomore year at a selective four-year college, and seeks assistance at the counseling center for symptoms related to anxiety.

The examples given below from oral feedback scripts and written reports are only brief excerpts, but they illustrate the principles covered while showing the recommended tone and style. In addition, for ease of presentation, I have acted as though only a single professional is providing feedback. In many settings, teams perform evaluations, and the guidance below can be adjusted in such a situation.

The Oral Feedback Session

At the oral feedback session, typically no other professionals are present besides you and possibly fellow members of your evaluation team. On rare occasions, a client or parent will bring a practitioner who is already treating the examinee, but the target audience is still the client or family. Therefore, the emphasis must be on providing a nontechnical description of test results and one that connects with other data. Remember that the feedback session is a clinical interaction as well; just as you would pay attention to your dress, your nonverbal behavior, your wording, and any emotional displays during clinical assessment itself, doing so during a feedback session will make the session more likely to be successful.

Particularly if you are a student in training, or perhaps an early career professional, try to write out your feedback before the first time you have such a session. Do not actually read the "script" aloud at the session; write out the feedback to ensure that your thoughts are organized and that you are happy with your phrasing. Write it in conversational language, as you would when you speak naturally, rather than writing it as you would for a formal report. If possible, show a draft to a colleague, classmate, or supervisor. As you get additional experience with feedback sessions, consider still having at least a broad outline written down to make sure you remember to cover everything. When a feedback session is interactive (as the best sessions are), it is sometimes easy to lose track of the most important information you wish to convey, unless you can refer to an outline.

Reiterate Referral Concerns

Start by reminding the client or family why the evaluation was conducted in the first place. If it was at their behest, it is especially important to check your notes from the intake referral. The primary concerns reported on one particular day may not be prominent in the audience's mind during the feedback session. Therefore, if you jump quickly into test results, the audience may not understand why those particular results are especially relevant. Going over the referral concerns can also be a way to convey empathy and confirm understanding of the perspective of those who referred the examinee.

Even though the referral concerns should never come as a surprise at an evaluation feedback meeting, reiterating them can come off in some cases as overly negative. Depending on the exact nature of the concerns, as well as your audience, you may want to mix information about the concerns with comments about the examinee's strengths. You don't want to seem flippant or unaware of the severity of the concerns (particularly if the client or family has mentioned feeling that their concerns were not being taken seriously enough). Instead, you want to acknowledge that the examinee is multidimensional and that their weaknesses do not define them.

> **Case A:** *(to Ashante's mother)* When we first met, you mentioned that Ashante seemed distracted a lot of the time. Even though she's a really positive young

lady—very extraverted, very excited—the inattention was getting to be a real problem. She seemed to be daydreaming even when you were trying to tell her important things like who would pick her up from school on a particular day. We talked about how you have a nephew diagnosed with ADHD, and you were wondering if Ashante might also have something like that.

Case B: *(to Blake's parents)* You might remember that Blake's teacher, Ms. Robbins, was concerned about his reading progress. He didn't finish up first grade on target for where his reading skills should have been, and I think you had gotten his state test scores in the mail—he was below the basic level in reading. He seems to be trying really hard, so Ms. Robbins wasn't worried about anything behavioral or any motivation problems. We just really needed to see if there was something going on that was causing problems for him learning to read.

Case C: *(to Carmen's parents)* I know that you were especially interested in Carmen's speech development. If I remember correctly, you really started to notice at family gatherings that Carmen wasn't talking nearly as much as some of her younger cousins, and even some of your family members were asking if something was wrong. I really focused our testing around issues of speech to figure out, first, whether she was on track for her age, and second, if she wasn't on track, why that might be the case. It was a pleasure to work with her—she's such a happy girl. Even though she doesn't say much, she's always smiling and laughs a lot!

Case D: *(to Daiki)* When we met a couple of weeks ago, you started off by telling me about how much time you were spending worrying. It felt like you weren't able to get much work done, and I know that this was particularly a problem near the end of the semester, with final exams and project due dates on the horizon. You'd been getting very high grades, you mentioned, but it seemed like it was only at great expense, since the pressure to do well was always on your mind.

Describe the Assessment Procedures Used

At a feedback session, you want to convey confidence in your conclusions and recommendations. A way to help the audience share your confidence is to emphasize the thoroughness of the evaluation you performed. Do *not* try to dazzle the audience with technical terms or list the official names of the tests you gave. Instead, describe the different assessment tools (not just tests), and for the formal tests, describe the types of tasks and/or the skills and traits they are designed to measure. Explicitly connect the assessment tools to the referral questions; explain *why* you used these tools. Emphasize that you followed standard evaluation practices, that this is how the particular referral questions in this evaluation are typically addressed in an evidence-based way. The more you demonstrate that you were consistent with generally accepted assessment procedures, the less you need to defend the procedures.

There is generally no need to give psychometric information about the tests. However, if the audience has questions, it may be helpful to provide such information. For instance, if a parent asks you how you know that their child had below-average levels of math skills, you could explain in general how norm-referencing works: *We compared Sally to a lot of other children her age—a group of children drawn from all across the country who took the same diagnostic test—and her math reasoning skills were in the bottom 10% of that group.*

You also should generally avoid mentioning actual test items. This is particularly true for performance measures (e.g., cognitive, achievement, neuropsychological tests). Disclosing actual test items can compromise test security, or it may lead the audience to focus too much on a specific item or two, which they then might take issue with (e.g., "Well, of course she doesn't know the meaning of *sunrise*; she's only seven, and she's never up early enough to see one!"). Instead, give an example of the item style or format but something that is not actually on the test. On measures of personality and psychopathology, mention individual items only if they are "critical items"—items containing content that is so significant that the item responses can stand alone as indicators of significant risk or a need for further inquiry (e.g., an item on a depression scale related to suicidal plans).

Case A: ADHD is a neurological disorder, but it can't be diagnosed based on a blood test or a brain scan. Instead, we use a mixture of observation, interview, and different behavioral measures. So that's why, when we met, I asked you a bunch of different questions about ADHD symptoms, and I also asked you some questions about other problems to help rule out different disorders. I also interviewed two of Ashante's teachers. You remember that I asked you to fill out a questionnaire about Ashante, and I did the same thing with a similar questionnaire for those two teachers. Before I even met Ashante, I actually went to her math class to observe her behavior during a lesson, just to see for myself if she seemed engaged throughout the lesson. And then I met her to interview her directly and asked her to take a test on my computer—a set of tasks where she needed to try to keep paying attention to different numbers on the screen and press different keys depending on what numbers she saw. Finally, I went to Ashante's cumulative file and looked at her report cards going back to kindergarten; in particular, I looked at her teacher comments and ratings for behavior and work habits.

Case B: When a student is having reading problems, we typically do testing for a learning disability in reading. So we assess reading skills definitely, but we also assess other things that could be causing a learning disability, and we try to rule out other problems too. So our school psychologist gave Blake an IQ test just to check on Blake's general cognitive skills—thinking skills, memory, things like that. I gave Blake a few different reading-related tests and I also gave Blake a couple of brief measures of writing skills, including spelling. Students who have learning disabilities that affect reading often have writing problems too. And finally, I interviewed you both and also Blake's teacher to learn more about exactly what problems you all see, and to learn more about Blake as a person, to find out what's he's good at as well as where he's struggling.

Case C: To see if Carmen's speech development was on track, I started by visiting your home, and I got to see Carmen playing with her older sister, Maria. I was watching to see what Carmen's speech was like in her natural environment, at home. When you visited our clinic, I gave Carmen a test of language skills that had a few different speech-related tasks. For instance, I showed Carmen some pictures of different objects and asked her to tell me what they were. I also interviewed both of you about what Carmen's development has been like since birth, to get a sense of how her language understanding and use has progressed. My colleagues and I also gave Carmen some other tests to measure her general cognitive skills, to see how well she understands other people's speech, and to rule out other problems.

Highlight Any Data that the Audience Contributed

If you employed rating scales, questionnaires, or interviews with the client or informants present for the feedback session, make sure to review the data from those tools, and consider mentioning them prior to other assessment results. This shows the audience that you clearly paid attention to the audience as a source of valuable information and that you weighed that information substantially when drawing conclusions.

Focus on Qualitative Ranges and Percentiles

Numbers are the stock-in-trade of assessment professionals, but they do not come easily to all laypeople. Therefore, focus on the qualitative ranges of test scores, even the broadest, crudest range labels. Be as precise as you need to be but no more than that. When covering performance measures, you can sometimes stick to "above average," "average," and "below average." This is especially relevant in areas that were not a particular focus of the assessment, where you were simply screening to confirm that there were gross deficiencies. On measures of personality and psychopathology, the same broad ranges are helpful, but make clear that "above average" means more severe problems on (for instance) a measure of ADHD symptoms, rather than indicating that the examinee is functioning better than most peers.

When appropriate, give more precise qualitative ranges. This is especially relevant when describing areas of extreme problems or deficiencies. When justifying a conclusion of "severe" anxiety or of intellectual disability or another condition that requires very deviant scores, it is important to make clear that the examinee is not a borderline case. Range descriptors such as "very low" or "extremely low" can be helpful; just make clear that you're applying them to particular scores and not as generalized descriptions of a person.

When there is a need for more precision, particularly when describing areas where problems or deficiencies are present, offer percentiles whenever possible. However, make sure to explain what percentiles are, and explicitly state that they are *not* percent correct scores. It can be helpful to describe a percentile as placing the examinee in the top or bottom 5 or 10 or 20% of people in their age group (or whatever normative comparison is used), since this cannot be confused with percent correct. Percentiles, like any other score type, are not free of measurement error, but they are nonetheless easier to understand intuitively, compared to many other norm-referenced scores.

Case B: On one test, I showed Blake a list of words that started out with very easy ones and got a bit harder as the list continued. He had trouble on this test; his score was below average, and it was obvious that he was struggling to read the words, even ones that most first graders can read without trouble. We're able to stop the test after he gets several words wrong, so the test didn't go on for too long. His score was actually in the bottom 5% of kids his age. I also gave him a test where I'd say two words to him and ask if they rhymed—some of the pairs sound similar but don't rhyme, words like "speed" and "speak." Even though he didn't need to read anything on that test, we know that a lot of students with reading disabilities have difficulties with this task, since reading requires a good understanding of the sounds that make up words. Blake did have trouble here too—his score was below average, in the bottom 15% of kids his age.

Case D: I asked you to complete a questionnaire about things related to anxiety, and your scores show how you compare to hundreds of other college students across the country. One of the scores was about worrying—the problem that you mentioned initially. When it came to worrying, your symptoms were definitely above average; your score was actually in the top 5% of college students. Another score was about physical symptoms of anxiety, things like a racing heartbeat. Here your symptoms were also above average but less severe; your score was in the top 15% of students. Finally, some of the items asked about whether you have a tendency to avoid things that cause anxiety. On that part of the questionnaire, your score was actually in the average range, and that's good news, in a way. This shows that you're motivated to do things that you need to do—things like finishing a paper assignment—even if those things cause you a lot of anxiety.

Place Test Scores in the Context of Other Data

Always emphasize **convergent evidence**—assessment data from different sources that point toward the same conclusion. At times this can be done across different types of test scores, such as when two different measures of the same construct are given to the same person. At other times, the convergence will exist across a test score, interview data, behavioral observations, and reviewed records. As a clinician, you generally wouldn't make a decision regarding diagnosis or recommended treatment on the basis of a single test score, and so it's important to let the feedback audience know the full complement of evidence that led you to your conclusions. This also helps to guard against pushback or genuine uncertainty on the part of clients and families; single pieces of evidence can be explained away, but a network of evidence from different sources is much more difficult to resist.

Convergent evidence is important, but so is acknowledging substantial discrepancies between data sources. Although few clinical cases are true "gray area" cases, it is also rare that *all* of the evidence points in the same clear direction, at least with regard to the precise level of functioning or severity of problems. Some amount of variability across measures is the rule, not the exception. Work to score measures early, to identify discrepancies before an evaluation is complete; this way you can administer more measures if necessary, go back to interview sources to ask additional questions, and so on. When discrepancies occur, look carefully at the different measures to develop hypotheses as to why they diverged, and discuss the hypotheses with the most evidence behind them at the feedback session. If a particular data point seems to go against your diagnostic conclusions, explain why you're drawing the conclusions in spite of that data point.

Case A: Your ratings of Ashante's inattention symptoms were very high; you actually placed her in the top 2% of children her age in terms of the severity of her problems. I asked her language arts and science teachers to complete similar rating scales, and both described her inattention symptoms as being above average, although it seemed that the problems were much worse in language arts. I know that Mr. Warren, Ashante's science teacher, has a really interactive class with lots of lab activities most weeks, and so this might help to engage Ashante better, or possibly Mr. Warren isn't as able to keep an eye on her and notice every symptom as well as if it were a traditional lecture-based class. When I went to observe Ashante in math class, she did seem to be paying attention, but I happened to visit the class during a small group activity where the teacher was working with Ashante's table. When she took the computerized test of attention in my office, it was easier to see her distractibility; she found the task very difficult, and her overall score was in the bottom 1% of students her age. So most of this evidence points in the direction of significant problems with attention. It seems that Ashante can attend better when in small-group, interactive environments where she's actively involved in activities, but in other, more typical settings, she does have significant problems paying attention, compared to the vast majority of her peers.

Case C: When I came to your house and observed Carmen playing with Maria, it was obvious that Carmen almost never speaks. Maria seems to not even expect Carmen to speak; whenever Maria asked Carmen a question, Maria would almost immediately answer it for her. The preschool language measures that I gave Carmen at our clinic also showed delays in speech development. On the formal tests of speech, Carmen never used full sentences. Sometimes she gave individual word answers that were correct, but she had trouble with certain sounds—for instance, when she encountered "k" sounds, she usually replaced them with "t" sounds. Overall, her expressive language score—basically, her speech development score—was at the 5th percentile for her age. That means that her score was near the lowest 5% of her agemates; it was among the lowest performance that we see in children her age. On an articulation test that measured her ability to

Sharing Test Results 147

produce sounds correctly, she didn't get several of the sounds that most 4-year-olds typically get. All this also goes along with what both of you had noticed informally and mentioned when I interviewed you. There are some other language tests that I gave of what we call receptive language—the ability to listen and understand other people's language—and her scores here were definitely higher; most were in the average range. So it looks like there are definitely problems with speech, but thankfully they don't extend to any consistent problems with listening.

Conclude with Any Diagnoses and the Most Important Recommendations

The oral feedback session proceeds by recapping the steps of the evaluation in roughly the order in which they happened. You had started by reiterating the referral information, you described what assessment tools were used and what their results were, and now you conclude with the inferences that you made on the basis of those results.

Just as you did when describing the assessment procedures, try to note that your conclusions are in line with official guidance and accepted procedures in the field. When you diagnose a disorder or say that a client qualifies for a special education category, note that you're following the official criteria (or legal regulations) for diagnosis or identification. When you make recommendations for treatment, remediation, management strategies, or accommodations, mention any guidelines that you're relying on, and note that your recommendations are in keeping with typical, standard practices. Your written report may have pages of recommendations; the oral feedback session is a time to emphasize the most important ones that can be followed up on immediately.

When issuing diagnoses, be aware that the audience can perceive a diagnosis as a prognosis—an expected course and outcome that's quite negative. Try to normalize the diagnosis by emphasizing its common nature (if appropriate), and make sure to note the availability of effective treatment/management strategies.

Case B: When our team considers whether a student has a learning disability, we start out by looking for academic skill problems that are causing poor educational performance in at least one academic area. Blake clearly has consistently low reading scores on formal tests, and they go along with low language arts grades in class. We also try to rule out other problems that could explain this. Blake has good attendance, seems motivated, and we've been providing informal reading help (the small-group reading remediation twice a week) that hasn't helped much. On an IQ test, all of his scores were in at least the average range, and a few were actually above average, so mental ability isn't a problem for him. Blake meets the state regulations and district guidelines for a learning disability in reading. Learning disabilities actually make up the largest category of students receiving special education, and that's the service we're recommending for Blake. That way, we can offer more resources and special instruction than can be done informally. Our school reading specialist will meet with him three times a week for reading instruction and exercises to help get him back on track, particularly with his ability to sound out words fluently—accurately and automatically.

Case D: Based on the questionnaire that you completed, as well as the information that you shared in the interview, you meet the official criteria for generalized anxiety disorder or GAD, which is really a way of saying that you have really excessive worries that are causing significant problems for you. You've been unsuccessful in controlling the worries, and they've caused problems with concentration, sleep, and fatigue. This level of worry has been going on for several months, and it's not due to a different problem like drug use. These are all the criteria for GAD. The good news is that psychotherapy can be very helpful in treating GAD. Several types of therapy have been shown in research studies to significantly reduce symptoms, and more importantly, therapy has helped many people be more effective and accomplish goals in spite of whatever anxiety remains. Some people with GAD also benefit from medications; I see that you have a regular GP, and you might want to speak with her about this. You can share my report with her, and if you sign a release giving me permission, I'm happy to speak with her myself so that we can put our heads together to offer you the best advice about which treatments to pursue first.

Solicit Questions and Take Them Seriously

Early in the meeting, make sure to ask the audience if there are any questions, and ask them to stop you at any point if questions arise. You don't want to ever get very far into a mass of information that the audience doesn't understand. It's easy to use a technical term without realizing it or to skip over a step when describing the logic for your conclusions. Therefore, periodically pause and ask whether the audience has any questions, and whether what you've said makes sense.

Questions that are simply informational (e.g., being asked to define a technical term) are easy enough to handle. If your audience poses more critical questions, seeming to doubt any of the evaluation data or the logic going from that data to conclusions and recommendations, don't become defensive. Thank the person for their question, acknowledge that they've raised an important issue, and address it carefully and patiently.

> **Case B:** It's a fair point that you raise about Blake's performance on the other reading fluency test that I gave—Blake did manage to get a score there at the bottom of the average range. It's possible that the words on that reading list had more overlap with the relatively few words in Blake's sight-word vocabulary. In total, the tests of reading-related skills that I administered generated over a dozen scores, and all of the others besides that one were below average. It was important to me to go with the weight of the evidence; all students show some variability across measures, but I definitely wouldn't want to withhold interventions based on that one score, when the vast majority of the evidence is telling us that there are problems.
>
> **Case D:** It's a good question that you're asking, about disability accommodations for classes and specifically deadline extensions. Although you certainly meet the criteria for generalized anxiety disorder, your record shows clearly that you do well in classes without accommodations—it's just a stressful experience for you. More importantly, anxiety isn't generally a sound basis for accommodations. In the short term, accommodations can take some pressure off and make you feel better, but the accommodations won't do anything to help you learn how to handle the anxiety, and in the long run, accommodations can actually make anxiety worse.

A Special Topic: Making No Diagnosis

Some diagnostic assessment books seem to assume that every examinee has some type of disorder, and the purpose of the evaluation is to identify *which* disorder is present. This is not the case. The threshold for performing an evaluation is that there is a *concern* about someone; sometimes the evaluation finds that the concern is unfounded or that it is due to an issue other than a disorder. When this occurs, particularly if the concern is unfounded, the evaluation feedback meeting can be awkward. Hearing that "everything is ok" is not always welcome news when someone is experiencing distress or seeking services. Objective diagnostic test scores can help to assure examinees and families that the decision not to diagnose is the right one, but the concern still needs to be addressed. If you are going to imply that someone's concern is unfounded, you need to explain why the concern was likely present in the first place. Similarly, if someone's functioning is impaired by an external factor (e.g., stress, a mismatch between abilities and goals, unreasonable expectations, relationship problems) rather than a disorder, that factor must be identified in the feedback so that the audience will know what to attribute the concern to.

Consider alternate versions of two of the cases described above, where the assessment data do not support a diagnosis, and excerpts from how a clinician might give that feedback:

Case A: I know that you've been noticing distractibility and daydreaming in Ashante. The rating scale that I asked you to complete compares Ashante to hundreds of students her age, and relative to that group, she's actually in the average range for inattention. Her score was in the middle 50% of students her age, not too high and not unusually low. You indicated how frequently she shows inattentive behaviors, and she does show some, but it appears to be only the amount that's typical for students her age. The teacher ratings actually show the same thing, and Ashante did well on the computerized test of attention that I gave her too. I know that this might be surprising, maybe even a bit hard to believe. Based on our interview, I think there are a couple of things that might be going on that explain the source of the concern that you had. For one thing, Ashante has to shoulder a lot of responsibility for a 12-year-old. For instance, you mentioned that she makes and packs lunch for herself and her siblings every morning before leaving for school, and then after school she needs to supervise her siblings doing their homework while she does her own. She might have attentional skills that are average for her age but that aren't sufficient for those responsibilities.

Case B: Our testing confirmed that Blake does have deficits in reading skills. Whenever that happens, our evaluation team needs to consider what has caused the deficits before identifying a student as having a learning disability. In Blake's case, as you know, he missed a lot of school this year due to illness. I know that he was out for most of October and November when he was in the hospital, and even after that, he wasn't really able to attend school consistently. We can't identify a learning disability if a student wasn't exposed to consistent instruction. Now that his medical issues have resolved, he wouldn't qualify for special education services for a physical disability either. But he has deficits in reading that we're committed to addressing. What we'd like to do is work with you to see if we can supercharge his reading instruction to get him back on track. The school year is almost over, but we'd like to give you a series of reading activities for the summer that either of you could do with him or that you might want to look into a tutor for. Next year, we would put Blake into our Academic Intervention Services program where he would go with two or three other children to the reading specialist for his reading period instead of staying in his regular classroom. Again, we don't think that this is a disability issue per se; there's nothing wrong with the way that Blake's brain works that prevents him from learning reading in the normal way. Instead, it's an instructional issue, and we want to do whatever we can to help resolve it.

The Written Report

The written evaluation report is very different from an oral feedback script. It is a permanent record, a document that may well be used in legal or regulatory proceedings and that may still be consulted many years after it is written. In addition, the audience for the written report goes far beyond the examinee and family members. Written reports are very often read by fellow professionals who are familiar with the technical aspects of diagnostic testing, and the needs of this audience should be considered when composing a report. While the oral feedback session should be nontechnical and consumer-friendly, when writing the written report, the needs of clients and families must be balanced with the goal of providing enough detailed information that other professionals can find out what they need to know from the report.

Guidance for report writing is plentiful and varied (again, see Appendix A). Depending on the setting in which you work, your reports may need to follow a certain format, and you may even contribute to joint reports from evaluation teams. Much of the discussion of oral feedback above can also be applied to written reports. Below I focus on the unique aspects of written reports that describe test performance, and I offer options and suggestions while acknowledging that their feasibility depends on the setting.

Early On, List All Tests Given

Many evaluators list all of the measures that were administered near the beginning of the report. This can be a vertical list or a block paragraph where the test names are separated by semicolons. For instance:

ASSESSMENT MEASURES

Clinical Interview

Wechsler Adult Intelligence Scale, Fourth Edition (WAIS-IV)

Wechsler Individual Achievement Test, Fourth Edition (WIAT-IV)

Nelson–Denny Reading Test, Form I (NDRT)

Conners Adult ADHD Rating Scale, Self-Report: Long Version (CAARS-S:L)

Conners Adult ADHD Rating Scale, Observer-Report: Long Version (CAARS-O:L)

Review of Educational Records

Note that the editions, versions, and forms of tests are stated clearly and explicitly. For instance, the current edition of the Nelson–Denny Reading Test has two parallel forms, I and J. If another professional were to be reevaluating a student who recently completed Form I, they might want to give Form J instead to reduce practice effects. The abbreviations of tests are given as well, so that you can feel freer to use the abbreviations without explanation later in the report.

Providing a list of all measures given near the beginning of a report serves two functions. First, it points to the comprehensiveness of your evaluation; it shows that you're not making important decisions on the basis of a single assessment tool. (In private practice settings where clients are paying directly for services, the list shows the amount of time that you put into the assessment.) Second, it provides an easy reference for fellow professionals. If I'm reviewing a psychological evaluation report, I often want to know if achievement tests were given; I can simply look down the list near the beginning of the report to see whether this is the case, and then I might skip ahead to glance at the results from those tests, before going back to read the report in full. If I'm reviewing an assessment report from a counselor and there are statements regarding the client's self-reported depression symptoms, it can be difficult to tell if those statements came from an informal interview or a standardized self-report questionnaire of depression symptoms; the list of measures administered helps me to figure this out.

Choose a Format for Organizing Test Data

There are three general formats for organizing test score data in the main body of the report. The first and likely the most common format uses the tests themselves to arrange the information. For instance, in the list used in the "Measures Administered" example in the previous section, the WAIS-IV data might be presented first, followed by the WIAT-IV data, the NDRT data, and so on. Each test would get its own heading to reinforce this organization. A second organizational strategy is to arrange the data based on functional domains, skills, or other traits measured. For instance, if all of the data from "reading skills" measures were presented together, the reading scores from the WIAT-IV would be presented in the same section as the NDRT scores; the other WIAT-IV scores (e.g., math scores) would be presented elsewhere. This strategy is seen in many neuropsychological reports, where all of the data related to a particular neuropsychological function (e.g., executive functioning) is presented together, even if the data is compiled from different test batteries, self-report questionnaires, and interviews. A final strategy is to present the data in response to posed "evaluation questions." For instance, in Case A (Ashante) from the first part of the chapter, a primary evaluation question is "Does Ashante have ADHD?" and others might be "Does Ashante have academic skill deficits?" and "Does Ashante need classroom or testing accommodations?"

The choice between the three general formats really involves choosing a balance between information that is helpful to clients/families and information that is helpful to fellow professionals. The first format is most helpful to fellow professionals, who are familiar with the tests and might prefer to make their own judgments regarding which tests measure which constructs and which diagnoses and recommendations are appropriate. The third format is very consumer-oriented, developed to make things clearest to laypeople. Finally, the second format is somewhere in between. Many examiners straddle the twin goals of accessibility and communication with other professionals by organizing the main body of the report around tests, but then making the final sections of the report ("Summary and Integration"; "Diagnostic Formulation"; "Recommendations") very consumer-oriented. Alternatively, the examiner can make the body text consumer-oriented but add an appendix of all test data, organized by test.

Levels of Detail

Reports vary widely in the level of detail of test score data reported in the body text. Consider a brief narrative description of intelligence test score data found in the main body text of a report from the psychoeducational evaluation of a high school senior:

> Janay was administered the Wechsler Adult Intelligence Scale, Fourth Edition (WAIS-IV) to assess her cognitive abilities in a variety of areas. Her Full Scale IQ (overall general cognitive ability score) was 115, better than 84% of people in her age group and in the high-average range. Her verbal comprehension index score, measuring things like her vocabulary and general fund of knowledge, was 120, better than 91% of people her age and in the superior range. Her perceptual reasoning index score, measuring things such as her ability to think in terms of visual and spatial relationships, was 107, better than 68% of people her age and in the average range. Her working memory index score, measuring her ability to store and manipulate multiple pieces of information at the same time, was 110, better than 75% of people her age and in the high-average range. Finally, her processing speed index score, measuring her ability to perform simple tasks quickly and accurately, was 108, better than 70% of people her age and in the average range.

That summary, in 174 words, describes the five composite scores of the WAIS-IV, what they measure (very briefly), the standard scores, percentile ranks, and qualitative ranges. This could be described as a "bare-bones" test performance narrative. What would some evaluators add?

1. Subtests—Each index score is based on multiple subtests, and some evaluators would add each subtest, with a brief description of the task or skills thought to be measured by the subtest, the score, and a qualitative range for the score. Other evaluators would relegate subtest data to a table, perhaps in an appendix.

2. Confidence intervals—No score is perfectly reliable, and confidence intervals (Chapter 4) help to reinforce that point. Such intervals are often available in scoring manuals and in computerized scoring programs, and while 90% confidence intervals are perhaps the most popular, others can be calculated as well.

3. More interpretation—To say that Janay's "ability to think in terms of visual and spatial relationships" is in the average range will not be especially meaningful to many readers. Some evaluators would discuss what kinds of classroom tasks Janay would be able to tackle using visual-spatial abilities, what everyday life activities depend on such abilities, and perhaps even what future college majors or career choices depend on such abilities (Janay is a high school senior, after all). Other evaluators only provide such "deep interpretation" in a summary/integration section at the end of the report; an argument for doing this is that it is difficult to interpret tests in isolation.

4. A table of scores—Some evaluators prefer to present small tables along with each narrative section; for Janay's narrative, the corresponding table is shown in Table 8.1. Other evaluators prefer to append all tables at the end of the report and leave the main body text for narrative only.

5. Graphs—A relatively small proportion of evaluators use graphs to supplement their presentation of scores. This typically involves a type of bar graph showing where scores fall relative to different ranges. In one study, Miller and Watkins (2010) found that parents were more satisfied with reports that had added graphs of test data and also recalled more information from such reports. I have used the style of graph that they used (more or less), to represent Janay's WAIS-IV data in Figure 8.1.

There is no single right answer as to whether these additions should be in your reports. When deciding which (if any) to include, consider the likely audience(s) for the report, the conventions in your profession and the setting in which you are working, and what your colleagues and supervisors recommend and why.

TABLE 8.1. **A Tabular Presentation of Janay's WAIS-IV Scores**

	Standard Score	Percentile	Range
Full Scale IQ (FSIQ)	115	84	High average
Verbal Comprehension Index (VCI)	120	91	Superior
Perceptual Reasoning Index (PRI)	107	68	Average
Working Memory Index (WMI)	110	75	High average
Processing Speed Index (PSI)	108	70	Average

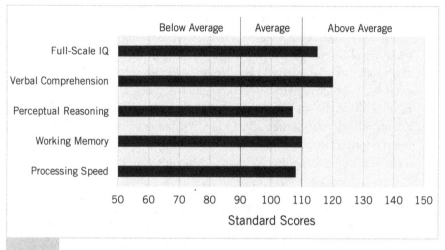

FIGURE 8.1. A graph showing Janay's WAIS-IV performance.

The Issue of Qualitative Ranges

As I discussed in Chapter 3, there is no single, universal set of agreed-upon qualitative range classifications for scores. There is an element of arbitrariness in determining whether a standard score of 88 is average or low-average, for instance. Worse still, different tests recommend different range cutoffs. For this reason, many evaluators choose a single classification system and present it in the report, often at the beginning of a test score appendix. Such an approach has much to recommend it; it keeps readers from being confused by seeing the same score on two different tests classified in two different ways. Let me add that for scores from tests that lack normal distributions, it is important to focus on the percentile score when determining the qualitative classification; on these tests (e.g., rating scales of psychopathology), the ranges may be different than for performance tests. This all can be presented and explained along with the scores in the report. A typical explanation, often presented before the score appendix, is the following:

Below are listed all diagnostic test scores from the present evaluation. Unless otherwise noted, measures of cognitive, language, and academic skills are interpreted according to the following system:

Standard Score	Scaled Score	Percentile	Interpretation
130 and above	16 and above	98th and above	Well above average
120–129	14 or 15	91st–97th	Above average
110–119	12 or 13	75th–90th	High average
90–109	8–11	25th–74th	Average
80–89	6 or 7	9th–24th	Low average
70–79	4 or 5	2nd–8th	Below average
69 or less	3 or less	2nd or below	Well below average

Unless otherwise noted, measures of emotional and behavioral problems are interpreted according to the following system:

Percentile	Interpretation
98th or above	Severe symptoms
93rd–97th	Clinically significant symptoms
84th–92nd	Above-average symptoms
83rd or below	No clinical concerns

(The second system has percentiles that correspond to cutoffs at 1, 1.5, and 2 standard deviations above the mean.)

The Evaluation's Conclusions

Typically, after presenting the results from all of the different assessment tools, reports include (1) a summary and integration of those results with additional interpretation, (2) a diagnostic formulation or statement of what criteria for different classifications the examinee meets, and (3) recommendations for treatment, accommodations, and other responses to the diagnoses and referral concerns. Obviously, doing this requires clinical expertise in whatever professional field the evaluation took place. My purpose here is to discuss how and when to cite assessment results (including test score data) in these concluding sections of the report.

The Clinical Summary

When providing a summary and integration, start by mentioning what concerns were present at the time of referral. Then, emphasize patterns of convergence and divergence in evidence, just as you did in oral feedback. For instance, if a structured interview, the rating scales from two respondents, and the results of a computerized test all point to significant ADHD symptoms, note this convergence, since it will increase your confidence (and the reader's) in the coming diagnostic formulation. If divergence is found, discuss the most probable reasons for it, and do so in a way that shows readers why some data sources may be less relevant or valid than others on specific points. Throughout the summary, whenever possible, emphasize the broadest composites and the overall classifications from measures. (This will prevent reliability issues from leading to apparent divergence, a common problem with subtest-level interpretation.) Most of the time, numerical scores can be left out of the summary entirely, with qualitative ranges standing in for them. Finally, to be maximally accessible, the summary should generally leave out the names of tests.

How much time should be spent reviewing test performance in the summary? The length of the summary will be proportional to the length of the full report, but two factors should be considered when deciding how much detail to provide in the summary: (1) whether the testing showed any clinically significant findings and (2) whether the testing was related to specific referral concerns. If a test shows nothing clinically significant and was only given to ensure a comprehensive evaluation of functioning, a sentence may suffice. Sample excerpts from summary statements follow:

- *An intelligence test showed average-range cognitive functioning in all areas.*

- *An intelligence test showed a high-average overall IQ, with some variability across sections.*

- *An intelligence test showed an average overall IQ, but consistent with referral concerns, Mara's working memory score was in the below-average range; her ability to temporarily hold and manipulate information in her mind appears to be impaired.*

- *On a test of language development, Isabella's receptive language (listening comprehension) was consistently average, but her expressive language scores were more variable, and her ability to verbally describe pictures that she saw was well below the average range.*

- *On self-report scales of depression and anxiety symptoms, Thomas did not report clinically significant problems.*

- *Thomas reported clinically significant problems on a self-report scale of depression symptoms; his score was in the range of a depressive disorder with moderate severity.*

The Diagnostic Formulation

In the diagnostic formulation section, consider explicitly referencing test score data to justify the formulation. For instance, the clinical diagnostic criteria for a learning disability require that someone have below-average academic skills relative to age-based norms. The criteria actually recommend an academic achievement score on a diagnostic test at least 1.5 standard deviations below the mean (American Psychiatric Association, 2013). It is helpful to reference the test scores showing that this standard is met, as you make the diagnosis. More often, in educational settings, legal or regulatory standards are cited; the state guidelines for diagnosing a learning disability or for declaring a preschooler disabled often have quantitative standards, and citing relevant test scores can be helpful here too. Generally, it is a poor idea to force the reader to go through the entire report to see what justifies the diagnosis or special education classification.[1] Sample diagnostic formulations follow.

- *The data from this evaluation are consistent with the diagnosis of intellectual disability under the current edition of the* Diagnostic and Statistical Manual of Mental Disorders *(the DSM-5). There is evidence that Mara meets all of the criteria for that disorder:*

  o *On the Wechsler Intelligence Scale for Children, Fifth Edition (WISC-V), her Full Scale IQ was 58.*

---

[1] Of course, in many cases, a particular diagnosis or educational classification requires that an examinee meet standards that go beyond specific test scores. In such cases, other information—perhaps obtained through clinical interview, observation, or record review—should be mentioned as well when making a diagnostic formulation or a conclusion about what educational classification criteria are met.

○ On the Vineland Adaptive Behavior Scales, Third Edition (Vineland-3), she showed significantly below-average functioning in the areas of receptive communication, expressive communication, play and leisure, and coping skills.

○ She is only 5 years old, meeting the age-of-onset criterion.

• The data from this evaluation are consistent with the diagnosis of major depressive disorder, moderate (DSM-5 296.22; ICD F32.1). There is evidence that Thomas meets all of the criteria for that disorder:

○ During a structured clinical interview (the SCID-5), he reported experiencing the following symptoms nearly every day for (more than) the past two weeks: depressed mood, loss of interest/pleasure, insomnia, fatigue, and feelings of guilt and worthlessness.

○ The symptoms are causing considerable distress as well as impairment in the workplace and in interpersonal relationships (e.g., with his wife). On the Barkley Functional Impairment Scale (BFIS), Thomas and his wife both rated his impairment in several areas as being in the moderate or severe ranges.

○ The symptoms are not due to a medical condition (e.g., thyroid problems have been ruled out) or drug use.

In some settings—particularly in some schools—individual evaluators do not make diagnoses or educational classifications, as these decisions are left to teams. In such cases, the reports can skip this subsection or else mention categories "for consideration."

Recommendations

Finally, test score data can be used to support specific recommendations for interventions, accommodations, and resources. It is often appropriate to cite such data explicitly, particularly if recommendations are likely to be controversial, expensive, or not followed for other reasons. Say that parents refer their teenage daughter for a psychoeducational evaluation due to concerns about a learning disability because of the amount of time she spends studying and preparing for tests. The evaluation finds average or above-average academic skills in every area, but also very high (clinically significant) levels of anxiety. The parents seem to be resistant to this reconceptualization of their daughter's problems, even though the parents' own symptom ratings of her showed high anxiety. As an evaluator, you want to document that you recommended counseling or psychotherapy for anxiety, including some specific behavioral techniques related to the content of the girl's worries. Citing the data from the anxiety measures (including the parents' own ratings but other data as well) in the recommendations section of the report can be helpful. Indeed, often initial resistance wanes over time, and the parents will be able to go back to the report later and consider your comments in a different frame of mind.

Citing testing data can also be helpful when making recommendations that do not flow directly from the diagnostic formulation. When an examinee's symptoms or impairment are unusually severe or atypical even relative to other individuals with the same diagnosis, the testing data can help to explain your individualized recommendations.

Sample recommendations that come with mention of test data are as follows:

- *It is recommended that Mateo's ADHD symptoms receive immediate intervention. The evaluation found that he not only met the criteria for ADHD but had severe symptom levels (scores above the 99th percentile from both parent and teacher report). His disruptive behavior is causing significant difficulties at home and especially at school. It is recommended that Mr. and Mrs. Diaz consider consulting with a health care professional about the possibility of medication for ADHD and that they also consider enrolling in a parent training program for behavior modification procedures tailored to children with ADHD. The Northside Community Center (phone: 212-555-2934) offers an 8-week program for parents locally.*

- *It is recommended that Angela receive individualized 1:1 reading skill remediation. Although she has already received some intervention in a school resource room setting three days per week, her reading skills remain significantly below age expectations on diagnostic tests. On the Woodcock–Johnson IV Tests of Achievement, her ability to decode individual words (on the Letter-Word ID test) was in the 5th percentile, and her fluency (on the Sentence Reading Fluency test) was in the 2nd percentile. These scores are similar to those obtained on the same tests one year ago, suggesting that different—and likely more intensive—intervention is warranted.*

- *It is recommended that James spend time with his high school counselor exploring careers related to mechanical skills. Not only are his skills quite good (his mechanical aptitude on the Differential Aptitude Tests Mechanical Reasoning test was at the 95th percentile, relative to other high school seniors), but on the Strong Interest Inventory, his highest score was in the "Realistic" area, which corresponds to many jobs involving mechanical skills.*

Conclusions

Tests are administered, scored, and interpreted by assessment professionals, but *sharing* the test scores (and other assessment data) with other people is the first step in actually solving the problems that are brought to us. Often, we initially share data through oral feedback, and when done well, such feedback can actually itself be therapeutic. Assessment data can confirm long-held suspicions, explain vague distress, and give a name to problems that have been poorly understood. Data can also provide relief and reassurance by ruling out problems. As a necessarily brief encounter, the oral feedback session must focus on the most important assessment results and their implications. Oral feedback is typically followed by a written report providing far more detail, including any information that the evaluator wants in the permanent record that will be seen by other professionals. Information about tests and test scores has a place throughout the report and is particularly worth mentioning when justifying conclusions regarding diagnoses and recommendations. This also shows readers that there is a clear connection between all of the measures that you administered and scored and the implications for the examinee; it justifies the use of the measures as much as it does your conclusions.

APPENDIX A

Resources for Further Study

Practical Psychometrics is designed to be an introduction—possibly a test user's first experience with some of these concepts. I had to make many difficult decisions about what to include and what to omit, and my hope is that many readers will go on to learn about psychometrics in greater detail. This appendix is an annotated guide to resources for further study in psychometrics. It also serves as a bibliography of sorts. Although I cite references throughout the book for specific points, there are times when I consulted the following sources as well.

General Textbooks

Many general textbooks in psychometrics treat the subject with more statistical rigor and simply provide more detailed coverage of these topics. I would recommend either of these two recent volumes as great "next steps " for readers:

- Bandalos, D. L. (2018). *Measurement theory and applications for the social sciences.* Guilford Press.
- Furr, R. M. (2018). *Psychometrics* (3rd ed.). SAGE.

Bandalos's book is extremely comprehensive, providing a resource that could be used for a year-long course just on psychometric theory. Furr's book is briefer but still rigorous. Both books use real-world test data to illustrate points. In addition, two earlier books are still quite useful, although they are perhaps a bit more difficult to find:

- Allen, M. J., & Yen, W. M. (1979/2002). *Introduction to measurement theory.* Waveland.
- Crocker, L., & Algina, J. (1986/2006). *Introduction to classical and modern test theory.* Cengage.

Finally, let me recommend an interesting book that applies psychometrics to clinical situations, particularly to clinical decision procedures:

- Haynes, S., Smith, G. T., & Hunsley, J. D. (2019). *Scientific foundations of clinical assessment* (2nd ed.). Routledge.

Haynes and colleagues cover some of the same psychometric ground that I do, but with more technical rigor and a specific focus on clinical psychology.

Another General Resource

Three professional associations—the American Educational Research Association (AERA), the American Psychological Association (APA), and the National Council on Measurement in Education (NCME)—have collaborated for decades to develop standards for tests. The most recent (2014) edition of their standards is available for free download here:

- *www.testingstandards.net/open-access-files.html*

Personally, I find the standards more useful for test developers than for test users, but there is certainly information of interest there for everyone, and some of the standards cover issues about test use in particular settings (such as educational settings).

Statistical Concepts

Most introductory statistics textbooks do a nice job covering in (much) greater detail the concepts I covered in Chapter 2. It is generally important to go through a statistics textbook in a linear fashion because topics build on each other, and new symbols and terminology are introduced in each chapter. (*Note:* The symbols often vary somewhat from one book to another; be careful with this!) Personally, I am partial to Barry Cohen's books—for example:

- Cohen, B. H. (2013). *Explaining psychological statistics* (4th ed.). Wiley.

However, again, most introductory statistics books do a fine job. Do make sure you use a book that covers effect sizes; most do now, but a few are still stuck in old ways of statistical analysis that only use p-values.

I can also recommend a more advanced book on correlation and regression that makes a lot of connections to psychometrics:

- Bobko, P. (2001). *Correlation and regression* (2nd ed.). SAGE.

The Bobko book requires background from an introductory statistics course, but it is an excellent second step in learning about statistics that are especially relevant to testing.

Test Score Interpretation

Despite the importance of the topic, it is difficult to find good general resources on test score interpretation that cover the information from Chapter 3 in greater detail. An exception is the recent chapter on "The Meaning of Test Scores" in this recent textbook:

- Reynolds, C. R., Altmann, R. A., & Allen, D. N. (2021). *Mastering modern psychological testing: Theory and methods* (2nd ed.). Springer.

Reynolds and colleagues discuss some of Chapter 3's topics and a great deal of other interesting information as well. I also recommend this excellent chapter from an edited anthology:

- Brooks, B. L., Sherman, E. M. S., Iverson, G., Slick, D. J., & Strauss, E. (2011). Psychometric foundations for the interpretation of neuropsychological test results. In M. R. Schoenberg & J. G. Scott (Eds.), *The black book of neuropsychology: A syndrome-based approach* (pp. 893–922). Springer.

Brooks and colleagues cover more advanced information and particularly address how to interpret test scores that change over time.

Finally, a now-classic article addresses a common clinical assessment situation that relates to issues of test norms:

- Bracken, B. A. (1988). Ten psychometric reasons why similar tests produce dissimilar results. *Journal of School Psychology, 26*(2), 155–166.

Bracken discusses how even surprisingly large differences between an examinee's scores on two similar tests can often be easily explained by the way that the tests' norms were constructed.

Reliability

Reliability is covered well by general psychometrics textbooks. However, one issue worth mentioning here is the interpretation of Cronbach's alpha, perhaps the most widely used reliability statistic. In recent years, alpha has come under severe attack from some psychometricians, who have proposed alternate ways of determining the internal consistency of tests. Although most diagnostic test developers and manuals continue to use alpha, an increasing number of researchers are using alternatives. To learn more about this debate and the new procedures that are available, I recommend the following articles:

- McNeish, D. (2018). Thanks coefficient alpha, we'll take it from here. *Psychological Methods, 23*(3), 412–433.
- Raykov, T., & Marcoulides, G. A. (2019). Thanks coefficient alpha, we still need you! *Educational and Psychological Measurement, 79*(1), 200–210.
- Sijtsma, K. (2009). On the use, the misuse, and the very limited usefulness of Cronbach's alpha. *Psychometrika, 74,* 107–120.

These papers are best tackled *after* reading the sections on reliability in one of the general psychometrics textbooks mentioned above.

Finally, item response theory (IRT) is covered well in separate chapters of the general psychometrics books recommended in the first section above. However, if you have a particular interest in IRT, you may find this conceptual introduction helpful:

- Hambleton, R. K., Swaminathan, H., & Rogers, H. J. (1991). *Fundamentals of item response theory*. SAGE.

Validity

Validity is actually a rather neglected topic in many psychometrics textbooks, which focus only on its technical, statistical aspects. Different scholars define validity in different ways, and a nice compilation of fairly recent perspectives on validity is available in:

- Lissitz, R. W. (Ed.). (2009). *The concept of validity*. Information Age.

For those seeking an interesting historical approach to the evolution of ideas about validity in assessment, try:

- Newton, P. E., & Shaw, S. D. (2014). *Validity in educational and psychological assessment*. SAGE.

Both of these books represent the views of many major scholars and have references to the journal articles where those views were first presented (often with more technical detail).

Finally, for those interested more in the validity concepts related to clinical classification, most of these concepts are *not* covered well in psychometrics textbooks, but they are handled with both clarity and detail in Chapters 20 through 30 of:

- Mayer, D. (2010). *Essential evidence-based medicine* (2nd ed.). Cambridge University Press.

Factor Analysis

I recommend two resources (beyond the general psychometrics textbooks) to learn about factor analysis in greater detail:

- Meyers, L. S., Gamst, G., & Guarino, A. J. (2017). *Applied multivariate research: Design and interpretation* (3rd ed.). SAGE.
- Pett, M. A., Lackey, N. R., & Sullivan, J. J. (2003). *Making sense of factor analysis*. SAGE.

The Meyers and colleagues book is a general textbook on multivariate statistics, with paired chapters on each statistical procedure. One chapter in each pair explains the conceptual background of the procedure, and the other chapter gives step-by-step instructions on how to perform the procedure (mostly using the statistics software SPSS). There are a few sets of chapters on different factor analysis procedures. The Pett and colleagues book is substantially more advanced, but it moves slowly enough that if you devote time to going through it, you will really understand the math behind factor analysis and how to make decisions if you choose to do a factor analysis (as well as making informed judgments about others' factor analysis results).

Bias and Fairness

For all of the claims made in the popular media about biased tests, not many books on the topic offer sound, research-based information. However, I can recommend an edited anthology that does directly take on some media claims and covers testing across many different settings:

- Phelps, R. P. (Ed.). (2009). *Correcting fallacies about educational and psychological testing.* American Psychological Association.

A second edited book on fairness issues specifically in educational assessment is worth reading, and it contains a balanced set of perspectives:

- Dorans, N. J., & Cook, L. L. (Eds.). (2016). *Fairness in educational assessment and measurement.* Taylor & Francis.

Finally, since no other recent books are available on the topic, I will eschew modesty and recommend my own book on testing accommodations, for readers more interested in fairness toward examinees with disabilities:

- Lovett, B. J., & Lewandowski, L. J. (2015). *Testing accommodations for students with disabilities: Research-based practice.* American Psychological Association.

Communicating Test Score Information

There is no shortage of books on report writing, but I will start by recommending an interesting book that contains many sample reports as well as information about how to write the different sections of a report, with specific guidance depending on the type of case (e.g., disability type) being considered:

- Dombrowski, S. C. (2020). *Psychoeducational assessment and report writing* (2nd ed.). Springer.

Dombrowski's book is most valuable for practitioners in school psychology and special education, but those in other fields can also read the book with profit.

Two other books that readers in various fields may find helpful regarding report writing are:

- Hass, M. R., & Carriere, J. A. M. (2014). *Writing useful, accessible, and legally defensible psychoeducational reports.* Wiley.
- Stein-Rubin, C. & Fabus, R. (2018). *A guide to clinical assessment and professional report writing in speech-language pathology* (2nd ed.). Stack.

Finally, although it is specifically from the field of neuropsychological assessment, I recommend this excellent book on oral feedback regarding evaluation results:

- Postal, K. S., & Armstrong, K. (2013). *Feedback that sticks: The art of effectively communicating neuropsychological assessment results.* Oxford University Press.

Answers for Applied Exercises

Chapter 2

1. You might say to your colleague: the standard deviation is a measure of how spread out test scores are, so test scores with a standard deviation of 10 are not spread out as much as scores with a standard deviation of, say, 20. You can also think of the standard deviation this way: if you picked a score at random, how far away from the average would it be? In this case, a typical randomly selected score would be 10 points away from the average. Since in this case we also know the mean (an average, 50) as well as the standard deviation, we know a few more things: about two-thirds of people (technically, about 68% of people) will have scores between 40 and 60 on this test, the vast majority of people (about 95% of people) will have scores between 30 and 70, and only about 2% of people will have scores either below 30 or (another 2%) over 70. Moreover, virtually everyone (about 99.7% of people) will have scores between 20 and 80 (i.e., within 3 standard deviations of the mean).

2. One way of interpreting a correlation coefficient is to square it, yielding the coefficient of determination. .60 squared is .36, suggesting that 36% of the variability in people's job satisfaction is attributable to their degree-of-match to their job as assessed by this personality test. Another way of interpreting a correlation coefficient is to test its statistical significance. Here, the p-value is .01, which is below the typical threshold for significance, .05, meaning that this relationship is statistically significant. Really, this means that if there were no relationship in the population

as a whole, it is very unlikely that a sample of 500 people would show a correlation of .60 or greater. A final strategy for interpreting the correlation coefficient is to compare it to Cohen's reference standards. In this case, the correlation is in the "large" range, even greater than Cohen's "large" reference standard of .50. We can conclude that the relationship between degree-of-match scores on this test and job satisfaction is statistically significant and large.

3. Cohen's d for these data would be calculated as the difference between the two groups (85–78 = 7) divided by the standard deviation (in this case 18). The d-value would be 7/18 = 0.389. This is not a statistically significant difference according to the p-value, which is .08 (above .05).

Chapter 3

1. Here are typical interpretations of the scores in the table:

   a. Intelligence—verbal, Standard Score of 115—this would be above the average range (in what is sometimes known as the high-average range), at approximately the 84th percentile, exactly one standard deviation above the mean. This would appear to be a strength for the adolescent.

   b. Intelligence—nonverbal, Standard Score of 103—this would be in the average range, at approximately the 58th percentile, one-fifth of a standard deviation above the mean. This area of performance is unimpaired, at the very least.

   c. Reading—reading individual words aloud, a Subtest scaled score of 8—this would be in the average range, at approximately the 25th percentile, two-thirds of a standard deviation below the mean. This area of performance is unimpaired but lackluster, perhaps something to monitor.

   d. Reading—answering comprehension questions, Subtest scaled score of 11—this would be in the average range, at approximately the 63rd percentile, one-third of a standard deviation above the mean. It is another unimpaired area.

   e. Math—performing calculations, Subtest scaled score of 5—this would be below the average range, at approximately the 5th percentile, one and two-thirds standard deviations below the mean. This would be an area of weakness, suggesting significant problems for the student.

f. Math—application/word problems, Subtest scaled score of 7—this would be below the average range (in the low-average range), at about the 16th percentile, exactly one standard deviation below the mean. This would be an area of potential mild weakness.

g. Parent-report of attention problems, *T*-score of 62—this would be in the high-average range at about the 88th percentile, a little more than 1 standard deviation above the mean. This student's parent-reported attention problems are certainly higher than those of most students, but they are perhaps not in the clinical range (which typically requires a score at the 93rd percentile or above).

h. Parent-report of hyperactivity, *T*-score of 48—this would be in the average range at about the 45th percentile, very close to the mean. This would be an area of unimpaired functioning.

i. Parent-report of anxiety, *T*-score of 73—this would be far above the average range, at about the 99th percentile, more than two standard deviations above the mean. This would be an area of impairment, suggesting very high anxiety in the clinical range, more severe anxiety than 99% of students.

j. Parent-report of depression, *T*-score of 65—this would be above the average range, at about the 93rd percentile, one and one-half standard deviations above the mean, and at the threshold for clinically significant problems.

k. Parent-report of conduct problems, *T*-score of 34—this would be well below the average range, at about the 5th percentile. This student has far *fewer* conduct problems (at least as reported by their parent) than most students do, so this would in essence be an area of strength.

In sum the test data suggest that the adolescent has significant problems with anxiety, depression, and mathematics—particularly in the area of math calculation.

2. Just because Briana's age-equivalent score is a year below her chronological age, this doesn't have any implications for grade retention. It doesn't even suggest that her skills are significantly below average. At any given age, there is a wide range of student skill levels, and Briana's may still be in the average range; there's no way to know otherwise when looking at an age-equivalent score. Age-equivalent scores are supposed to indicate where the average (median) student at a particular age performs, but there may or may not have been actual children who had just turned 6 years old in the test development sample anyway. Rather than focusing

on age-equivalent scores, check the percentile rank to see whether Briana is substantially below average. (Even if she is, retention may be a poor idea as educational policy, which is a separate issue.)

3. Robert shows what happens as a student progresses through education and is compared to higher-functioning reference groups. In a community college, where there is more of a general population sample, Robert's performance was adequate but lackluster. When he transferred to a four-year college, he was being compared to a higher-performing sample, and his grades declined; as the standards went up, he had more trouble meeting them. His standard score of 87 in reading comprehension shows that his reading comprehension skills were at the 19th percentile (i.e., in the bottom 20%) of college juniors, and while we do not have information on his other skills yet, this is consistent with his poor grades. If he were compared to the general population rather than to college juniors, his standard score would likely be higher.

4. Whenever a testing battery generates several scores, there is a fair probability that at least one score will be very high or very low just by chance. Jane's single very high *T*-score may be real and meaningful, but additional evidence would be needed, since seven other scores seem to suggest a *lack* of clinically significant trauma symptoms. The high score should be taken as a hypothesis to be tested with other sources of information such as a clinical interview or record review. Of course, no clinical decision should ever be made on the basis of a single test score, but in this case, where only one *of several scores* was above a clinical threshold, even more care should be taken.

Chapter 4

1. Although there is a discrepancy between Janay's IQ (125) and her overall language development score (110), discrepancies are not especially reliable, particularly when the two tests making up the discrepancy correlate (as we would expect measures of IQ and language development to do). Another reason why the discrepancy would be poor evidence of a language disorder is that Janay's language development score is actually at the 75th percentile, on the border between the average and high-average ranges. Imperfect reliability is yet another possible explanation of this discrepancy, and calculating confidence bands for the two scores could help to examine this possibility. Finally, regression to the mean

may explain why the language score is closer to the mean than the IQ score is. In sum, it would be highly problematic to overinterpret the discrepancy, when there are so many possible explanations for it.

2. Because the internal consistency reliability coefficients of the TCI scores are so high (close to 1, between .90 and .95), they would typically be interpreted as having little error due to item content variability and as each measuring a unitary construct. (A factor analysis would be helpful in confirming this interpretation.) However, since the test–retest reliability coefficients are low (all below 0.5), this suggests that high school students' career interests tend not to be very stable over time.

3. The SEM values for the TRF scores are approximately as follows: Affective (Mood) Problems = 4.9, Anxiety Problems = 5.2, ADHD Problems = 2.4, Aggressive Behavior = 2.2. Manny received an Anxiety Problems score of 62 from his teacher, and the 95% confidence interval for this score is $62 \pm 2(5.2) = 62 \pm 10.4$. This means that Manny's true score might be anywhere from 62–10.4 (about 52) to 62 + 10.4 (about 72). This is a very large range, and one that suggests that no substantial decisions should be based on that score alone. In any case, a score of 62 is in a border region, clearly above average but not clearly in the clinically significant range.

Chapter 5

1. The TOMS is designed to measure math skills in middle school students. Therefore, construct underrepresentation would mean that some relevant math skills in middle school are not included sufficiently in the test items; those parts of the construct (middle-school-level math skills) are not represented sufficiently by the TOMS. Construct-irrelevant variance would mean that some of the items on the test include content or require skills beyond middle-school-level mathematics. Students' scores on the TOMS will then vary in part due to variability in these other, construct-irrelevant skills. In inspecting the items, a special education teacher might note whether all of the topics covered in middle school mathematics are found somewhere on the test, and whether the items require any skills (e.g., advanced vocabulary skills) beyond middle school mathematics. More generally, content-related validity evidence for the TOMS might include a review of state or national standards for middle school mathematics curricula, showing how all parts of those standards

are measured by various items on the TOMS. Relatedly, the TOMS manual might report the results of a study where experts in middle-school-level math education reviewed the items and rated them as relevant to measuring math skills in this population. Finally, for convergent validity, the TOMS developers might correlate scores on the test with scores from other standardized diagnostic tests of math skills (e.g., math scores from the Wechsler Individual Achievement Test).

2. The correlation between CAARS self and observer ratings of .49 is closest to convergent validity evidence. However, it could also be thought of as concurrent validity evidence, if observer ratings are regarded as a more objective criterion that self-ratings are predicting. The correlation would even relate to interscorer reliability from Chapter 4. However, convergent validity would be the type of *validity* evidence that this correlation is closest to; the two raters (the client and the person who knows them well) are thought of as offering descriptions of the client's ADHD symptoms that should *converge* on the same level of symptoms. Considering that different sources of information (the client and the observer) often differ in perspective, I would describe 0.49 as a "good" correlation, suggesting good validity evidence. This level of correlation has also been found in studies with other measures (which is helpful research to know about). The correlation could also be interpreted in terms of the coefficient of determination; about 24% (.49 squared) of the variability in self-ratings is explained by variability in observer ratings, and vice versa.

3. For this test, the sensitivity value is .96 (48/50) and the specificity value is .58 (29/50). This supports the use of the test for screening purposes, since screening tests should be highly sensitive, but their specificity is not as important because everyone who "screens positive" will be given a further evaluation. This is good classification validity evidence for this purpose, but the screener should not be used for diagnosis, given the poor specificity.

Chapter 6

1. The two verbal comprehension subtests (Similarities and Vocabulary) correlate at $r = .68$, and the two visual-spatial subtests (Block Design and Visual Puzzles) correlate at $r = .60$. Both of these correlation coefficients are higher than any of the correlations between any verbal comprehension subtest with any visual-spatial subtest (those cross-area correlations

range from .46 to .51). This would be *some* evidence for interpreting the Verbal Comprehension Index and Visual-Spatial Index scores separately. That said, the difference between the sizes of the two types of correlations (i.e., within-area correlations and across-area correlations) is not very large. This would suggest to some scholars that our emphasis should be on interpreting an overall score that is based on performance on all of the subtests. In fact, IQ tests such as the WISC-V also offer these overall scores, and practitioners can choose which scores to emphasize when making clinical interpretations.

2. There is no single "correct" answer to what factors should be named or what they represent. However, here is one analysis based clearly on the EFA data. Items 1, 3, 6, 7, and 9 of the AMAS all have far higher loadings on Factor 1 than on Factor 2, whereas items 2, 4, 5, and 8 all have far higher loadings on Factor 2 than on Factor 1. Looking at the item content, we find that items 1, 3, 6, 7, and 9 all describe activities that might happen during math *instruction* or *studying* math. Meanwhile, items 2, 4, 5, and 8 all describe activities related to math *tests*. This pattern suggests that anxiety about math instruction is partially separate from anxiety about math testing. Indeed, Hopko and colleagues (2003) named Factor 1 "Learning Math Anxiety" and Factor 2 "Math Evaluation Anxiety."

3. Four CFA fit statistics are given. The χ^2 value cannot be readily interpreted on its own; we would need the χ^2 value from another model to see if one is better than the other. Of the other fit statistics, the CFI and TLI are actually above the typical standards for "good" fit, and the RMSEA is in the "acceptable" range as well. It is also important to note that the test developers assessed this CFA model against another one and found that this model was significantly better. Overall, this is good, positive CFA evidence that supports the validity of interpreting the different scores (across subtests and forms) that the TOWRE-2 provides.

Chapter 7

1. With regard to predictive bias, you could search for studies of the MTOI's predictive validity (or even concurrent validity). For instance, perhaps there is a study using the MTOI to predict school grades; you could check if the regression lines for African American students and White students were the same or very similar for that type of prediction. With

regard to internal structure evidence of bias, you could search for studies examining the factor structure of the MTOI across different groups, making sure that the factor structure is essentially the same (i.e., that there is factorial invariance) across African American and other groups. Finally, with regard to DIF, you would do well to check the MTOI manual first, since DIF analysis may have been used to eliminate items through the process of test development. You could also search for independent research finding that the relationship between ability (intelligence) and performance on each MTOI item is the same across different groups.

2. The precise optimal response would differ depending on the information in the clinical inventory manual, as well as the nature of the client and client's mother, but a reasonable response might be: Girls do score somewhat higher on this scale of borderline personality traits than boys do, but that doesn't necessarily indicate bias. To check, we need to ask if adolescent girls might really have more of these traits, things like changing moods rapidly and feelings of being let down by friends. A number of research studies have found that these traits *are* actually more common in teenage girls than boys. In fact, feeling these things at least occasionally might be a typical part of adolescent development for girls. However, your daughter actually has a much higher score than other girls, and so that's one piece of evidence that I need to pay attention to when I make any diagnostic judgments and think about how to best work with her.

3. The question of whether and when a calculator is an appropriate accommodation on a diagnostic test relates to whether arithmetic calculation (i.e., the procedure that the calculator will do for the student) is a target skill or an access skill for each subtest. The Calculation subtest seems obviously to be designed to test calculation skills, meaning that a calculator would compromise the validity of the subtest rather severely. The Math Facts Fluency subtest also seems designed to measure math calculation skills. The Applied Problems subtest is the one where calculation skills are ambiguous, in terms of whether they are a target skill or an access skill; the best case for a calculator accommodation would be on this subtest. If a calculator accommodation is used on any part of a diagnostic test, it would be extremely important to note this in an evaluation report. Not only is this a deviation from standard test administration protocols, which would affect any norm-referenced scores generated by the test, but the inferences from scores from subtests taken with a calculator would differ. For instance, if the student received a standard score of 110 on the Calculation subtest when using a calculator, we could not

validly infer that they know how to perform the mathematical operations themselves, or even that they know basic math facts. The 110 score would be relative to students in the norm sample who did not get to use a calculator, so even the interpretation of the student having average/high-average math skills would not be appropriate.

4. If you are concerned about performance validity, you could administer a specialized assessment tool (a performance validity test) that would screen for effort. However, only some clinicians have training in administering these specialized measures. A less formal approach to assessing performance validity would compare the student's performance on the cognitive test that you're giving to other data regarding their cognitive skills. For instance, if the student obtains very low scores on the cognitive test, are there any prior evaluations showing how they performed in the past? Can you check with the student's teacher to see if their behavior during the testing session (e.g., the student's claims to not know the answers to certain questions) is plausible? Regardless, given your (reasonable) concerns about the student's performance validity, these concerns should be documented in the evaluation report, along with specific details of their behavior during testing.

Glossary

Access skills—the set of skills needed to fairly participate in a test under standard test administration conditions. Contrast with **target skills.**

Age-equivalent score—a test score indicating the age at which the median student received the same raw score as the examinee. Such scores are easily misinterpreted and not recommended for use in most cases.

Alternate form reliability—a **reliability** estimate calculated by developing two parallel forms of a test and correlating scores from one form with scores from the other form in the same sample of examinees.

Base rate—(1) the general prevalence of a condition in the **population** of interest or (2) the general prevalence of a certain test score value or pattern of score values in the population.

Bivariate descriptive statistics—statistics used to describe the relationship between two variables in data from a particular **sample.**

Classical test theory (CTT)—the set of statistical assumptions that guides psychometric work on most tests, starting with the assumption that any observed test score consists of a true score level and some amount of error.

Coefficient of determination (r^2)—the square of the **correlation coefficient**; typically interpreted as indicating the proportion of variability in one variable accounted for by variability in the other variable.

Cohen's *d*—see **Standardized mean difference.**

Cohen's kappa (κ)—an index of **interscorer reliability** that takes into account chance agreement between two judges.

Computerized adaptive testing—a testing procedure in which a test adapts to an examinee's responses, by (for instance) generating harder items if the examinee answers items correctly and generating easier items if the examinee answers items incorrectly.

Concurrent validity—a type of **criterion-related validity** evidence in which examinees' scores on a test correlate with their performance on another measure obtained at the same time.

Confidence bands—a visual representation of the range around an examinee's obtained test score, showing what range we can be confident that their true score level is within. Confidence bands are calculated using the **standard error of measurement.**

Confirmatory factor analysis (CFA)—a statistical procedure used in ways similar to **exploratory factor analysis** but with a specific internal structure of a test specified. A CFA procedure determines how well the data for a test (particularly the set of relationships between the test items or sections) match the expected, posited structure of those relationships.

Construct—an unobservable trait that is indexed using observable responses to test items. Examinees are expected to vary in their levels of the construct being measured. Examples of constructs include intelligence, reading skills, extraversion, and depression symptoms.

Construct-irrelevant variance—a type of validity problem in which some of the test items, or the testing process as a whole, measures traits other than the **construct** that the test is designed to measure.

Construct underrepresentation—a type of validity problem in which areas of the **construct** that a test is designed to measure are not represented in the test items.

Convergent evidence—in a clinical case, evidence from different sources that all points to the same conclusions with regard to diagnosis, identification, or recommendations.

Convergent validity—**validity** evidence in which multiple tests designed to measure the same or similar **constructs** correlate highly, converging on the same estimated construct level for an examinee.

Correlation coefficient (r)—a **bivariate descriptive statistic** that quantifies the strength and direction of the linear relationship between two variables. The correlation coefficient ranges from –1 to 1, with –1 indicating a perfect **negative correlation**, 1 indicating a perfect **positive correlation**, and 0 indicating no linear relationship at all between the variables. The most common correlation coefficient used is also known as a *Pearson coefficient*.

Criterion-referenced score interpretation—a type of test score interpretation that compares a person's test score to an absolute standard (or criterion) that is not dependent on how other people scored on the test.

Criterion-related validity—**validity** evidence based on correlations between scores from a test and another type of indicator (a criterion) that the construct measured by the test should be related to.

Cronbach's alpha—the most common measure of **internal consistency reliability**.

Descriptive statistics—statistics (such as the **mean**) used to describe a **sample**.

Deviation score—in a set of test scores, a deviation score is calculated for each score by subtracting the **mean** from it.

Differential item functioning (DIF) analysis—a statistical analysis used to determine if examinees from different groups have the same chance of responding correctly to a test item if they have the same level of the trait that the test is designed to measure.

Discriminant validity—a type of **validity** evidence in which tests designed to measure distinct, independent **constructs** should not correlate strongly with each other.

Effect size—a statistic indicating the size of a relationship between two variables, or the size of a difference between two groups that takes into account the amount of variability within each group.

Empirical rule—a description of the areas of different parts of the **normal distribution**. The rule states that in a normal distribution of test scores, approximately 68% of the scores will be within 1 **standard deviation** of the **mean**, approximately 95% of the scores will be within 2 standard deviations of the mean, and approximately 99.7% of the scores will be within 3 standard deviations of the mean.

Exploratory factor analysis (EFA)—a statistical procedure used to identify clusters of correlations among test items or sections of a test in an effort to identify the factors determining performance on the test items and better understand the internal structure of the test. In an EFA, no specific internal structure is specified prior to performing the analysis.

Face validity—a type of **validity** in which examinees who are taking a test (or other laypeople reviewing the test items) are able to determine what the test is designed to measure.

Factor loadings—in an **exploratory factor analysis**, factor loadings index the strength of a relationship between an item or test section and a factor. Higher factor loadings can also be viewed as showing that a factor has a stronger influence on performance on a particular test item or section.

Factorial invariance—a type of **measurement invariance** study result in which the internal structure of a test is shown to be similar for different groups using **confirmatory factor analysis**.

False negative—when a test indicates the absence of a condition but the examinee in fact has the condition.

False positive—when a test indicates the presence of a condition but the examinee in fact does not have the condition.

Fit index—in **confirmatory factor analysis**, fit indices show how well the data from a test fit a particular **measurement model**.

Frequency distribution—a figure, table, or graph showing how the values of a variable are distributed. It is typically graphed with the value of the score on the *x*-axis and the frequency of each score on the *y*-axis.

Grade-equivalent score—a test score indicating the school grade level in which the median student received the same raw score as the examinee. Such scores are easily misinterpreted and so are not recommended for use in most cases.

Histogram—the typical graph of a **frequency distribution**.

Incremental validity—the ability of a test to predict an outcome or criterion above and beyond other predictive information. For instance, if the SAT has incremental validity evidence above high school grades, the SAT would predict college performance even in a group of students with the same high school grades. The SAT would then be providing unique value. Incremental validity is typically assessed using **multiple regression**.

Inferential statistics—statistics used to make inferences about a **population** based on information from a **sample**.

Intercept bias—a type of **predictive bias** in which the two regression lines for two groups have different *y*-intercept values.

Internal consistency reliability—a **reliability** estimate based on the strength of the relationships between different items or other parts of a test. Stronger internal relationships suggest higher reliability.

Interscorer reliability—a **reliability** estimate based on how similar the scoring of different judges (test scorers, or raters) is for test responses from the same sample of examinees.

Item response theory—a set of statistical models developed in the past several decades to estimate examinees' ability levels based on how test items are answered and what properties (e.g., difficulty) each item has.

Mean (M)—a **measure of central tendency** calculated by summing all of the test scores in a sample and dividing by the **sample size**.

Measure of central tendency—a statistic used to represent a **sample** or **population** with a single value; often colloquially called an *average*.

Measure of dispersion—a statistic used to determine how spread out (or dispersed) the values of a variable are; also known as a measure of variability.

Measurement invariance—a type of statistical analysis using **confirmatory factor analysis** to obtain evidence of whether or not a test may be biased or may function differently in different groups. Specifically, if measurement invariance is found, this would be evidence against test bias.

Measurement model—the proposed internal structure of a test that is investigated with data using a **confirmatory factor analysis**. The confirmatory factor analysis may find that the data match the measurement model well or poorly.

Median—a **measure of central tendency** calculated by ordering a set of values of a variable from lowest to highest and finding the middle value.

Mode—a **measure of central tendency** calculated by identifying the most frequent value for a variable.

Multiple correlation coefficient (R)—a statistic generated by **multiple regression**; its square (R^2) is generally interpreted as indicating the proportion of variability in an outcome variable that is jointly accounted for by multiple predictors.

Multiple regression—a type of statistical analysis in which multiple predictor variables are used to estimate the value of an outcome variable.

Negative correlation—a relationship between two variables where as one variable increases, the other variable decreases.

Negative predictive value (NPV)—of those examinees who test negative for a condition, the percentage who in fact do not have the condition.

Norm group—the sample of people on which a test was standardized or "normed," to determine the distribution of typical examinees' scores, to allow for **norm-referenced score interpretations**. Also known as the standardization sample.

Norm-referenced score interpretation—an interpretation of test scores that involves comparison of one person's test score to other people's scores.

Normal distribution—a **frequency distribution** that is commonly found (in approximate form) for many types of test scores. When graphed, it resembles a symmetrical "bell-shaped curve." It follows a known mathematical function, and the area under different parts of its curve has been summarized by the **empirical rule**.

Norms—the distribution of a test's scores in the **norm group**; used to make **norm-referenced score interpretations**.

p-value—an indicator of **statistical significance** when using **inferential statistics**, with smaller p-values indicating more significant results. The p-value is the probability that a relationship between two variables as large or larger than the one found in the **sample** would have been found if there were no relationship between the variables in the **population** as a whole. By convention, a p-value below .05 is required for significance.

Percent agreement—an index of **interscorer reliability** calculated as the percent of judgments in which two judges make the same judgment.

Percentile rank—the proportion of the **population** that the examinee is estimated to have scored higher than.

Performance validity—a type of **response validity** specifically referring to the examinee putting forth adequate effort on cognitive tasks.

Population—a group of people who are of interest to a researcher or test developer; their characteristics are estimated using a **sample**.

Positive correlation—a relationship between two variables where as one variable increases, the other increases as well.

Positive predictive value (PPV)—of those examinees who test positive for a condition, the percentage who actually have the condition.

Predictive bias—a type of test bias in which the **regression lines** showing the relationship between test scores and a criterion are different for different groups.

Predictive validity—a type of **criterion-related validity** evidence in which scores from a test correlate with a future outcome for examinees.

Range—a **measure of dispersion** calculated by subtracting the lowest value of a variable from the highest value.

Raw score—the simplest type of score, based on the number of items answered in a particular way, number of points earned, or similar information from a test, before comparing the score to other people's performance.

Regression line—a line shown on a **scatterplot** that "best fits" the data. It is devised by finding the line that minimizes the distance from the line to all of the data points. Its equation can be used to predict the value of one variable given the value of the other variable.

Regression to the mean—a statistical consequence of imperfect test **reliability**, in which test scores that are far from the **mean** score are more likely to contain more error and the next test score examined is likely to be closer to the mean.

Reliability—the degree to which test scores are dependable and consistent across different items, different test forms, different scorers, or across time.

Response bias—insufficient **response validity**. Response bias compromises interpretations of an examinee's test responses due to potential problems with honesty, effort, or motivation.

Response validity—the property of test responses being accurate for the examinee, due to adequate honesty, effort, and motivation. Encompasses **performance validity** and **symptom validity**.

Sample—a group of people for whom we have data or test scores, which are often used to make estimates about a **population**.

Sample size (n, N)—the number of people (or the number of people's test scores) in a **sample**.

Scale—the range and distribution of a type of test score.

Scatterplot—a graph showing the relationship between two variables by plotting the value of one variable on the x-axis and plotting the value of the other variable on the y-axis.

Sensitivity—of those examinees who actually have a condition, the percentage who will test positive for the condition on a particular measure.

Sensitivity review panel—a group of diverse individuals who review test content to ensure that it would not be expected to be offensive to examinees.

Slope bias—a type of **predictive bias** in which the regression lines for two groups have different slopes.

Specificity—of those examinees who do not have a condition, the percentage who will test negative for the condition on a particular measure.

Split-half reliability—an estimate of **internal consistency reliability** calculated by dividing a test into two halves and correlating scores on the first half of the test with scores on the second half of the test in the same sample of examinees.

Standard deviation (SD)—a **measure of dispersion** calculated as the square root of the **variance**; commonly interpreted as indexing how far from the **mean** a typical score falls.

Standard error of measurement (SEM)—a statistic showing how much variability around an examinee's true score level would be expected, based on a test's reliability. The more reliable that a test is, the lower the SEM is, and vice versa. Based on the SEM, **confidence bands** can be calculated showing how likely it is that an examinee's true score level is a certain distance from the score that the examinee was observed to get.

Standard normal distribution—a **normal distribution** with a **mean** of 0 and a **standard deviation** of 1.

Standard scores—test scores from a distribution with a **mean** of 100 and a **standard deviation** of 15. Standard scores are used very frequently in diagnostic tests, and form the basis of most IQ scores.

Standardized mean difference (Cohen's *d*)—an **effect-size** statistic calculated by subtracting the **mean** of one group from the mean of another group and dividing that difference by an index of the within-group variability of the two groups.

Standardized regression coefficient (β)—statistic found in **multiple regression** indicating the strength of the relationship between a predictor variable and an outcome variable, when the values of the other predictors are held constant. It is used to indicate the *unique* value of each predictor. Technically, the standardized regression coefficient can also be used in simple bivariate regression, where there is only one predictor; in such a situation, it is equivalent to the **correlation coefficient**.

Stanines—test scores that range from 1 to 9, from a **normal distribution** divided into nine equal units.

Statistical significance—in **inferential statistics**, statistical significance is often used to indicate the confidence that we can have in making inferences about the **population** given the data in the **sample**. Statistical significance is typically quantified using a ***p*-value**; by convention, a *p*-value below .05 is required for significance.

Subtest scaled scores—test scores from a distribution with a **mean** of 10 and a **standard deviation** of 3. These scores are found on many tests of intelligence and adaptive behavior. However, note that subtests from some instruments generate scores that do not follow this distribution.

Symptom validity—a type of **response validity** specifically meaning that an examinee's symptoms were reported honestly and not exaggerated or inaccurately denied.

***T*-scores**—test scores from a distribution with a **mean** of 50 and a **standard deviation** of 10. These scores are common on measures of personality and rating scales used to measure behavioral and emotional problems.

Target skills—the set of skills that a test is designed to measure. Contrast with **access skills**.

Test–retest reliability—a **reliability** estimate calculated by administering the same test twice to the same sample of examinees and correlating examinees' scores from the first administration with their scores from the second administration.

Testing accommodations—alterations to the administration conditions of a test, to help individuals with disabilities access the test. Accommodations are meant to address deficits in examinees' **access skills** without changing the **target skills** needed to do well on the test.

True negative—when a test indicates the absence of a condition and indeed the examinee does not have that condition.

True positive—when a test indicates the presence of a condition and the examinee actually has that condition.

Univariate statistics—statistics based on a single variable rather than relationships between multiple variables.

Validity—the degree to which evidence supports interpretations and actions made on the basis of test scores. A valid test measures what it claims to measure, and valid interpretations and actions are supported by adequate evidence.

Validity coefficient—a correlation coefficient between test scores and another variable that are used as evidence of the test's **validity**.

Variance—a **measure of dispersion** calculated by finding the average squared **deviation score**.

z-score—a test score from a distribution with a **mean** of 0 and a **standard deviation** of 1. These scores come from the **standard normal distribution** and indicate how many standard deviations away from the mean a particular score is.

References

Achenbach, T. M., & Rescorla, L. A. (2001). *Manual for the ASEBA school-age forms and profiles*. University of Vermont.

ACT. (n.d.). *National norms for ACT test scores*. www.act.org/content/dam/act/unsecured/documents/MultipleChoiceStemComposite.pdf

American Psychiatric Association. (2013). *Diagnostic and statistical manual of mental disorders* (5th ed.). American Psychiatric Publishing.

Associated Press. (2021). NFL families seek to end "race-norming" in $1bn concussion settlement. *The Guardian*. www.theguardian.com/sport/2021/may/14/nfl-race-norming-concussion-settlement

Bandalos, D. L. (2018). *Measurement theory and applications for the social sciences*. Guilford Press.

Bennett, K. J., Lipman, E. L., Racine, Y., & Offord, D. R. (1998). Annotation: Do measures of externalising behaviour in normal populations predict later outcome? Implications for targeted interventions to prevent conduct disorder. *Journal of Child Psychology and Psychiatry and Allied Disciplines, 39*(8), 1059–1070.

Brooks, B. L. (2010). Seeing the forest for the trees: Prevalence of low scores on the Wechsler Intelligence Scale for Children, Fourth Edition (WISC-IV). *Psychological Assessment, 22*(3), 650–656.

Camilli, G. (2006). Test fairness. In R. L. Brennan (Ed.), *Educational measurement* (4th ed., pp. 221–256). Praeger.

Canivez, G. L., Dombrowski, S. C., & Watkins, M. W. (2018). Factor structure of the WISC-V in four standardization age groups: Exploratory and hierarchical factor analyses with the 16 primary and secondary subtests. *Psychology in the Schools, 55*(7), 741–769.

Cohen, J. (1988). *Statistical power analysis for the behavioral sciences* (2nd ed.). Erlbaum.

Conners, C. K., Erhardt, D., & Sparrow, E. (1999). *Conners' Adult ADHD Rating Scales.* Multi-Health Systems.

Dee, T. S., & Domingue, B. W. (2021). Assessing the impact of a test question: Evidence from the "Underground Railroad" controversy. *Educational Measurement: Issues and Practice, 40*(2), 81–88.

del Prado, A. M., & Church, A. T. (2010). Development and validation of the Enculturation Scale for Filipino Americans. *Journal of Counseling Psychology, 57*(4), 469–483.

Fishco, V. V. (2019). *Nelson–Denny Reading Test Forms I & J: Examiners manual.* PRO-ED.

Funder, D. C., & Ozer, D. J. (2019). Evaluating effect size in psychological research: Sense and nonsense. *Advances in Methods and Practices in Psychological Science, 2*(2), 156–168.

Green, K. L., Brown, G. K., Jager-Hyman, S., Cha, J., Steer, R. A., & Beck, A. T. (2015). The predictive validity of the Beck Depression Inventory suicide item. *Journal of Clinical Psychiatry, 76*(12), 1683–1686.

Guilmette, T. J., Sweet, J. J., Hebben, N., Koltai, D., Mahone, E. M., Spiegler, B. J., . . . Conference Participants. (2020). American Academy of Clinical Neuropsychology consensus conference statement on uniform labeling of performance test scores. *The Clinical Neuropsychologist, 34*(3), 437–453.

Gunzler, D. D., Perzynski, A. T., & Carle, A. C. (2021). *Structural equation modeling for health and medicine.* CRC Press.

Halpern, D. F., & Wai, J. (2020). Sex differences in intelligence. In R. J. Sternberg (Ed.), *The Cambridge handbook of intelligence* (2nd ed., pp. 317–345). Cambridge University Press.

Harrison, A. G., Butt, K., & Armstrong, I. (2019). Comparing age-and grade-based norms on the Woodcock–Johnson III Normative Update. *Educational and Psychological Measurement, 79*(5), 855–873.

Hartung, C. M., & Lefler, E. K. (2019). Sex and gender in psychopathology: DSM-5 and beyond. *Psychological Bulletin, 145*(4), 390–409.

Haslam, N. (2016). Concept creep: Psychology's expanding concepts of harm and pathology. *Psychological Inquiry, 27*(1), 1–17.

Hopko, D. R., Mahadevan, R., Bare, R. L., & Hunt, M. K. (2003). The abbreviated math anxiety scale (AMAS) construction, validity, and reliability. *Assessment, 10*(2), 178–182.

Hunsley, J., & Mash, E. J. (2008). Developing criteria for evidence-based assessments: An introduction to assessments that work. In J. Hunsley & E. J. Mash (Eds.), *Assessments that work* (pp. 3–14). Oxford University Press.

John, O. P., Naumann, L. P., & Soto, C. J. (2008). Paradigm shift to the integrative

Big Five trait taxonomy: History, measurement, and conceptual issues. In O. P. John, R. W. Robins, & L. A. Pervin (Eds.), *Handbook of personality: Theory and research* (pp. 114–158). Guilford Press.

Keith, T. Z. (2019). *Multiple regression and beyond* (3rd ed.). Routledge.

Li, C., Friedman, B., Conwell, Y., & Fiscella, K. (2007). Validity of the Patient Health Questionnaire 2 (PHQ-2) in identifying major depression in older people. *Journal of the American Geriatrics Society, 55*(4), 596–602.

Lovett, B. J., & Gordon, M. (2005). Test score discrepancies as a basis for the assessment of learning disabilities and ADHD. *ADHD Report, 13*(3), 1–4.

Lovett, B. J., & Lewandowski, L. J. (2015). *Testing accommodations for students with disabilities: Research-based practice.* American Psychological Association.

Lovett, B. J., Spenceley, L. M., & Lewandowski, L. J. (2022). Response validity in psychoeducational assessment: A primer for school psychologists. *Contemporary School Psychology, 26*, 279–289.

MacGinitie, W. H., MacGinitie, R. K., Maria, K., & Dreyer, L. G. (2002). *Gates–MacGinitie Reading Tests: Technical report for forms S and T.* Riverside.

Meyers, L. S., Gamst, G., & Guarino, A. J. (2013). *Applied multivariate research* (2nd ed.). SAGE.

Miller, J. A., & Watkins, M. W. (2010). The use of graphs to communicate psychoeducational test results to parents. *Journal of Applied School Psychology, 26*(1), 1–16.

Morgan, P. L., Farkas, G., Cook, M., Strassfeld, N. M., Hillemeier, M. M., Pun, W. H., & Schussler, D. L. (2017). Are Black children disproportionately overrepresented in special education? A best-evidence synthesis. *Exceptional Children, 83*(2), 181–198.

National Center for Health Statistics. (2021). *Anthropometric reference data for children and adults: United States, 2015–2018.* U.S. Department of Health and Human Services.

National Council on Measurement in Education. (2019). *Misconceptions about group differences in average test scores.* www.ncme.org/publications/statements/new-item2

Nelson, N. W., Plante, E., Helm-Estabrooks, N., & Holz, G. (2016). *Test of Integrated Language and Literacy Skills.* Brookes.

Rosenthal, R. (1990). How are we doing in soft psychology? *American Psychologist, 45*(6), 775–777.

Salo, S. K., Marceaux, J. C., McCoy, K. J., & Hilsabeck, R. C. (2022). Removing the noose item from the Boston naming test: A step toward antiracist neuropsychological assessment. *The Clinical Neuropsychologist, 36*(2), 311–326.

Schneider, W. J. (2013). Principles of assessment of aptitude and achievement. In D. Saklofske, C. Reynolds, & V. Schwean (Eds.), *Oxford handbook of psychological assessment of children and adolescents* (pp. 286–330). Oxford University Press.

Schrank, F. A., Mather, N., & McGrew, K. S. (2014). *Woodcock–Johnson IV Tests of Achievement*. Riverside.

Sireci, S. G. (1998). Gathering and analyzing content validity data. *Educational Assessment, 5*(4), 299–321.

Tiburcio, N. J., & Baker, S. L. (2020). *Estimates of the reliability and criterion validity of the adolescent SASSI-A3*. SASSI Institute.

Tombaugh, T. N. (1996). *Test of Memory Malingering*. Multi-Health Systems.

Torgesen, J. K., Wagner, R. K., & Rashotte, C. A. (2012). *Test of Word Reading Efficiency* (2nd ed.). PRO-ED.

Voyer, D., & Voyer, S. D. (2014). Gender differences in scholastic achievement: A meta-analysis. *Psychological Bulletin, 140*(4), 1174–1204.

Wechsler, D. (2014). *Wechlser Intelligence Scale for Children: Interpretive and technical manual* (5th ed.). Pearson.

Weiss, L. G., Locke, V., Pan, T., Harris, J. G., Saklofske, D. H., & Prifitera, A. (2019). Wechsler Intelligence Scale for Children—Fifth Edition: Use in societal context. In L. G. Weiss, D. H. Saklofske, J. A. Holdnack, & A. Prifitera (Eds.), *WISC-V Clinical use and interpretation* (2nd ed., pp. 129–196). Academic Press.

Whisman, M. A., Judd, C. M., Whiteford, N. T., & Gelhorn, H. L. (2013). Measurement invariance of the Beck Depression Inventory—Second Edition (BDI-II) across gender, race, and ethnicity in college students. *Assessment, 20*(4), 419–428.

Wiig, E. H., Semel, E., & Secord, W. A. (2013). *Clinical evaluation of language fundamentals* (5th ed.). Pearson.

Yoon, S., & Kim, Y. (2018). Gender differences in depression. In Y. Kim (Ed.), *Understanding depression* (pp. 297–307). Springer.

Index

Note. Page numbers in *italics* indicate a figure or a table.

About the Author

Benjamin J. Lovett, PhD, is Associate Professor of Psychology and Education at Teachers College, Columbia University, where he teaches courses in psychoeducational assessment, legal and ethical issues for school psychologists, and the history of psychology. He has over 100 publications, focusing on the assessment of high-incidence disabilities, the provision of testing accommodations, and the nature and management of test anxiety. A licensed psychologist, Dr. Lovett also serves as a consultant to schools and testing agencies on disability and assessment issues.